SS France/Norway

SS France/Norway

William H. Miller

The History Press

For one of the greatest maritime artists, especially for his work with ocean liners

DON STOLTENBERG

First published 2009

The History Press
The Mill, Brimscombe Port
Stroud, Gloucestershire, GL5 2QG
www.thehistorypress.co.uk

British Library Cataloguing in Publication Data.
A catalogue record for this book is available from the British Library.

ISBN 978 0 7524 5139 8

Typesetting and origination by The History Press
Printed in Great Britain

Contents

Acknowledgements

Although not the great size of the crew of a liner such as the *France*, it does take a considerable number of generously supportive, kind and very patient friends, fellow maritime historians and writers and, of course, ocean liner enthusiasts to prepare a book such as this. Anecdotes and insights have to be gathered and then the photos collected. Away from the project, they often anxiously await the publication of a book, much like shipyard workers look to the day of launching and then final completion. I am deeply grateful to all.

First class assistants on this project include Jane Bouche Strong, the late Frank Braynard, Tom Cassidy, Captain Cato Christensen, the late Captain Georges Croisile, Rebecca Cuxton, Bill Deibert, Richard Faber, the late Lewis Gordon, Michael Hadgis, Charles Howland, Abraham Michaelson, Captain Hans Meeg, Andre Morell, Captain Ed Squire, Frank Trumbour and Steven Winograd. Mostly for photographic assistance, the 'crew' deserving praise and gratitude include Ernest Arroyo, Philippe Brebant, the late Frank Cronican, William Donall, the late John Gillespie, Andy Hernandez, Pine Hodges, Norman Knebel, Peter Knego, Robert O'Brien, Fred Rodriguez, Jan Olav Storli, Kaushai Trivedi and Albert Wilhemi. Organisations that have assisted include the French Line, Norwegian Cruise Lines, the Port Authority of the New York & New Jersey, Steamship Historical Society, the World Ocean & Cruise Liner Society and the World Ship Society.

If, in error, I have failed to mention anyone, please accept my apologies as well as my extended thanks.

Introduction

On an otherwise cloudy, drab winter afternoon in February 1962, New York harbour was alive with excitement. Tugs hooted, fireboats sprayed and helicopters buzzed overhead. Exchanges of ships' whistles echoed throughout the port. The headline-making occasion was the maiden arrival of the spectacular French flagship *France*, the longest liner ever built (1,035ft overall), the latest transatlantic supership and – according to most early reports – the most luxurious liner then afloat. She moved slowly, with a sort of royal procession of tugs and other craft around her, to her berth on the north side of Pier 88, at West 48th Street. Later that day, a friend of my father's gave me the entire press packet, with glossy photos included, for the *France*. There was even a photo of the earlier, four-funnel *France*. He worked for US Customs and was a guest at an afternoon reception. That same week, I just added a replica of *France*, made in 1,250th scale and created by the Triang Company, to my fleet of miniature ships. (These days, I have over 1,000 of these cherished recreations in my collection, including one of the *Norway*.)

On a damp, rain-splattered afternoon in November 1963, I made my first visit to the remarkable *France*. She was at Pier 88, preparing for an evening departure for Europe, and the *Queen Mary* was nearby, at Pier 90. There seemed to be such an immediate contrast in appearance – the *Queen* was classic, traditional, the great three-stacker; the *France* was modern, different, trendy, so sleek and topped off by those exceptional funnels. A friend and I walked aboard, in what seemed to be a flood of fluorescent white light – up the gangway and into the entranceway and foyer – and then passed through the various public areas, into a world of varied colours and extremely modern furniture, at the time seeming to be a liner like no other. The tone of the French Line, that sense of ocean liner luxury and reminders of the likes of the *Normandie* and the *Ile de France*, the *Paris* and the *Liberte*, made the visit very special. There was also a great sense of excitement, but quiet excitement, about the ship and the people on board. It all seemed to run like a well orchestrated, perfectly directed script. It had this almost unruffled, but purposeful flow. You saw the passengers, the visitors, the staff and even the great stacks of luggage, but it was far quieter, or at least seemed to be, on board the *France*. So, you left feeling this elegance, like you had visited a fine hotel, museum or even a cathedral, because you had been aboard such an elegant vessel. A friend called it 'hushed elegance'. She was, based on that visit and long in memory, pure perfection. I also felt that while I missed seeing the exquisite *Normandie*, the new *France* was the greatest compensation. She was 'our *Normandie*' in the 1960s.

I knew well but was not quite fully aware just how much the great curtain had closed on the transatlantic liner business, but had at least some good sense and intuition to book passage in July 1973 for a summer visit to Europe on board the *France*. We left on a Thursday afternoon, on a classic five-day run over to Southampton and Le Havre. Again, you felt special, even if in lower-deck tourist class, to be sailing aboard the French Line. Again, there was this quiet excitement, a sense of hushed luxury, a gentle, almost whispered electricity. There were some 1,400 passengers on board, including some great loyalists who went back to the 1920s and '30s and who could rattle off just about every ship they had crossed in, as well as twenty-four dogs, eleven cats and three birds. Big American cars belonging to passengers had been loaded in the forward holds and, upon sailing, there was a small mountain of those classic steamer trunks, many of them in the chocolate brown of Vuitton. We had the most perfect weather – wonderfully warm with ink blue skies overhead and the calmest of Atlantic seas. The *France* rushed forward, doing something like 28 knots, but seemed to take possession of the sea rather than the sea of her. You could feel her great power, her weight, that indefinable might. There was also this great sense of purpose, of destination (so unlike today's slow-roaming cruise ships). Each of us had a deliberate reason for crossing on this fine ship. At Southampton, we made a brief call at the great deco-style Ocean Terminal and were in port together, in that final heyday of great passenger ships, with the likes of the *Windsor Castle*, the *Orsova*, the *Aureol* and the *Fairsky*. Later that afternoon, after docking at Le Havre, myself and so many others took the 'boat train' to Paris. I changed trains there later that night and was in Switzerland early the following morning. After some further travelling, I gradually wound my way down to Naples and caught the *Raffaello*, also in her twilight days, for a ten-night voyage home to New York. Crossing on these two great Atlantic liners was assuredly the highlight of that summer, of course.

I was also delighted to have made two Caribbean cruises on the *Norway*, one in January 1981 and the other in the summer of 1995. On the January trip, she was freshly converted, sparkling, exciting. She seemed in ways to be a very different ship, but still a very appealing one. It was an excellent transformation, a glorious remake from a basically indoor to a wonderfully outdoor liner. The second cruise showed, however, that the great ship was aging, dated, struggling even – the air-conditioning was inconsistent (and in the intensely humid summertime Caribbean no less), for example, and on board maintenance was not quite the perfection it had been. Nevertheless, it was again fascinating to sail aboard the former *France*.

Starting from her maiden arrival in New York back in February 1962, I have followed this exceptional ship's fortunes ever since. As I prepared this book, the forty-five-year-old liner was still lying, silent and waiting, on an Indian beach. Her time has come. But she has had a most successful and fortunate life, two noted careers and two highly recognisable names. She was one of the greatest of all twentieth-century liners. Hail to the *France/Norway*!

Bill Miller
Secaucus, New Jersey
Autumn 2009

one

French Line Heritage

'The French liners were the most beautiful and elegant of the 20th century,' felt Steven Winograd, a world-class ocean liner collector and devoted sea traveller. 'They were also the best fed and the best served. But with great beauty is also great fragility. French liners, it seemed, were stars that burned brightly, but then burned out quickly. Many had short lives, in fact far too short lives.'

CGT, the Compagnie Generale Transatlantique and quite simply the French Line to many, especially Americans, has a very long history. Today, it exists but as CGM, Compagnie Generale Maritime, and, since 1998, as CMA-CGM, mostly in container cargo shipping, but with some interests in leisure travel including a small French cruise firm. The company's prior history is long and extensive. The first French transatlantic passenger ship service actually began in 1847, seven years after Britain's Cunard Line and eight before Germany's Hamburg America Line, but then failed and was reorganised in 1855. It resumed as Compagnie Generale Maritime and was in the hands of two enterprising brothers, Emile and Isaac Pereire. Formidable, the new company had no less than seventy-six ships within a year and was trading to ports throughout the world. But the North Atlantic run from Le Havre as well as Bordeaux to New York drew the most attention. It was also the most competitive. By 1867, with the backing of the legendary Rothschild family, five fine new steamers were ordered especially for the increasingly competitive New York run. Encouraged, lucrative mail and operating subsidies were offered by the French government. By 1861, in yet greater force, the company was retitled as Compagnie Generale Transatlantique, CGT, or 'the Transat' as the French often dubbed it.

New tonnage, such as the 3,400-ton *Washington*, had to be built abroad, however – at a shipyard in Greenock in Scotland. With some embarrassment, the French themselves were not yet able to build such large ships. But again with the backing of the French government, a strip of land at the mouth of the Loire in an area known as Penhoet was purchased. A French shipyard, but with great help coming from the Scots, was developed. The first newbuild was the *Imperatrice Eugenie*, launched there in April 1864.

Profits grew steadily for CGT even if the Paris-based firm was more interested in first and second class passengers rather than the infamous, more lucrative steerage. CGT ships also carried the all-important mails. The company became interested not only in improved, even innovative passenger ships, with emphasis on shipboard comfort, even glossy luxury, but also in larger, more powerful ships. In 1876, for example, a CGT vessel was the first to have an on board 'lighthouse' (warning lights) and, as the Paris offices noted, 'potent fog horns'. That same year, the *Amerique* was the first electrically lighted steamer on the Atlantic. By 1891, with great success and profits continuing, the company added the 9,057-ton *La Touraine*, then the fifth largest passenger vessel afloat and, at 19 knots, one of the fastest. She was also well known, mostly in top travel circles, for her ornate, grand interiors as well as for splendid food. Cuisine became a hallmark on CGT liners. The Line also became noted for both reliability and continuity. By 1895, CGT posted schedules that provided a sailing from Le Havre to New York or vice versa every Saturday throughout the year.

Outbound from New York in the 1950s, the celebrated *Ile de France* was one of the most popular liners on the North Atlantic run. (Author's Collection)

By 1900, the company had added the 11,100-ton sisters *La Lorraine* and *La Savoie* and then, even bigger and grander and, of course, faster, the 13,700-ton *La Provence*. The latter had a very impressive 23-knot top speed, which cut the Le Havre-New York transits to six days. By 1909, and very much wanting to compete with the super liners of Cunard and Hamburg America, plans called for the largest French liner yet, the 23,600-ton, four-funnel *La Picardie*. She would be the ultimate French symbol of design, size, machinery and decor. She was also the great symbol of CGT's first half-century of success. When she went down the ways at Penhoet on a summer's day in 1910, and by which time she had been renamed *France*, she was in fact the beginning of a master plan of successively finer, larger liners for CGT.

'The glory of France' had to be seen on the high seas, specifically on the North Atlantic and amongst the other European liners then sailing. National prestige was very important. Subsequently, Parisian ministers were both very interested and very generous – they offered liberal construction loans as well as operating subsidies. In high enthusiasm, there was a general plan that called for a new French liner almost every four years.

An enhancement of the four-funnel *France*, the 34,500-ton *Paris*, whose construction was actually begun in 1913 but delayed by the First World War, was triumphantly added to the fleet in 1921. This time capped by three funnels, she was noted from the start for her sumptuous first class quarters and, once again, for her splendid food and service. Furthermore, especially to ocean-crossing Americans, the French liners seemed to have the greatest on board style and spirit. The French were said to offer 'the greatest and longest gangway to and from Europe'. Rightfully, the *Paris* was noted in the 1920s for having the fewest number of vacant berths in first class. She was hugely popular. She was a ship of film stars, midnight parties and masses of those Vuitton trunks.

Even if more moderate passenger ship tonnage was very much in vogue in the 1920s, the French opted next for an even larger, even grander liner. The 43,000-ton *Ile de France* was commissioned in 1927 and immediately captured the attention of not only Atlantic travellers, but the world. She was said to be the most luxurious liner of her day, the most innovative, the most original. She became the most successful and most beloved as well.

The late Frank O. Braynard, the noted American maritime historian, author and artist, said that:

No ship better typified the glamorous 1920s with all its bizarre modernism and hauteur than the *Ile de France*. She was consistently popular from the very start. When she first appeared, the French Line produced the most lavish descriptive folders and brochures detailing the wonders of the new flagship. One brochure, with a heavy gold cardboard cover, introduced the new liner as 'a bit of the mainland of France'. In it, regally stiff, short-skirted women pose in gaudy rooms, hold cigarettes and feather fans in an ostentatious manner and lead greyhounds around the Sun Deck.

The accommodations on the 791ft-long *Ile de France* were typically divided in three classes – first class, cabin class and third class. So comfortable, all cabins, even in inexpensive, lower-deck third class – had beds instead of bunks. Her first class quarters were exceptionally lavish and included a large assortment of suites and cabins de luxe. It was said to be the finest selection of top accommodations on the Atlantic. By 1935, the *Ile* had carried more first class passengers than any other Atlantic liner. Added Frank Braynard:

In July 1934, the *Ile de France* completed her first 100 roundtrips and carried 160,000 passengers in her seven years of service. This was an exceptional

Near the end, the glorious *Normandie*, seen here laid-up at New York on 16 May 1941, would be pathetically destroyed by a careless fire and capsized some nine months later, on 9 February 1942. (Frank O. Braynard Collection)

The brilliant *Normandie* departing from New York on her gala Carnival in Rio cruise on 6 February 1938. (Frank O. Braynard Collection)

average, especially in those otherwise lean Depression years, of 795 per crossing. Few ships could equal this mark. So popular, a large model of the *Ile* displayed at the Chicago World's Fair was said to be a top attraction.

Indeed satisfied, the French would continue to produce a parade of fine liners.

But it was the *Ile*'s overall decorative style, the beginning of Art Deco on the high seas, that captured the imagination of passengers as well as designers, decorators and even other, competitor shipping lines. Because of her, Art Deco became the new rage at sea. The earlier, heavily wooded, often cluttered style that often resembled shoreside sites was cast aside. Now, and prompted by the 1,786-passenger *Ile de France*, facilities on land began copying steamship decoration, 'ocean liner style' as it was called. Copied from the definitive Art Deco Exposition held in Paris in 1925, her interiors represented the new *moderne*. Almost single-handedly, she introduced the age of sleek, angular furniture, sweeping columns and panels, inventive lighting and a great sense of spaciousness. The first class bar was said to be the longest afloat and the first class restaurant, which rose three decks in height, was likened to a Greek temple. The main foyer was also three decks high and the chapel was done in Gothic and had no less than fourteen pillars.

While CGT created intermediate liners, such as the 17,000-ton *De Grasse* in 1924 and then the 13,300-ton *Colombie* in 1931 for service to the colonial French West Indies, primary planning and thoughts were still on the North Atlantic. The 25,000-ton *Lafayette* was added in 1930 and then, two years later, the 28,000-ton *Champlain*. That last named ship was said, in fact, to be a prelude to the giant, record-breaking liner the French were planning for the mid-1930s. She was also inspired by another French liner, the 42,000-ton *L'Atlantique*, completed in 1931 and which ran from Bordeaux to the East Coast of South America for another French passenger line, Compagnie Navigation Sud-Atlantique. The first keel plates for the new CGT behemoth were laid down in January 1931.

The 79,280-ton *Normandie*'s purpose was threefold: to be the world's largest liner (at over 60,000 tons and the first to exceed 1,000ft in length), to be the fastest on the Atlantic, and to be a dazzling floating centrepiece of, as CGT revealed, 'all that is France'. She would be the nation's finest ambassador and, despite the uncertainty of the Depression, would cost an extraordinary $60 million. She would be the ultimate ocean liner – advanced, exceptionally luxurious, a design and decorative tour de force. She succeeded on all counts.

'Few ships have impressed themselves so indelibly upon the common consciousness of our age as the great *Normandie*,' noted Frank Braynard. 'While she sailed for little more than four years, she so attracted [the] enthusiastic interest of the world that the extent of her influence on ship design, travel tastes, style, the movies and even toys is impossible to measure.'

The magnificent *Normandie* in a superb 1935 poster – note the deliberate reduction in the size of the New York harbour tugs so as to make the great liner appear even larger. (Author's Collection)

She had the most advanced appearance, capped by three large, but raked funnels. Her outer decks were all but swept clean of clumsy ventilators, booms and deckhouses. But it was her interiors, so resembling those used in Hollywood films at the time, that drew the greatest notice and highest praises. She was also exceptionally spacious and so possessed some of the largest and grandest lounges, salons – and even a first class main restaurant – ever to put to sea.

That main dining room aboard the *Normandie* was done in hammered glass, bronze and gleaming Lalique towers of light. Slightly longer than the famed Hall of Mirrors at Versailles, it sat 1,000 guests and rose three decks in height. The theatre was the first ever fitted to a liner and included a movie screen as well as a stage for live productions. The indoor pool was 80ft of tiled, graduating levels. The Winter Garden included exotic birds, abundant plant life and sprays of water. The main lounge was covered in Dupas glass panels. Each first class cabin was done in a different decor, resulting in 400 decorative themes overall. Two grand deluxe apartments headed the luxurious first class section and were placed on a secluded spot on the Sun Deck. Each had a private terrace (then a great novelty on board ships), four bedrooms, a living room, servants' quarters and a dining room that sat twelve and had a private pantry. Visitors rarely left the *Normandie* without being deeply impressed.

Some of the great names in French design and decoration – such as Dupas, Ruhlmann, Dunand, Subes and Lalique – were joined together to create the stunningly sumptuous *Normandie*.

Unfortunately, the *Normandie* had a very short commercial life. She was laid-up at New York in late August 1939, just as war clouds were forming over Europe. The French kept her at Pier 88 for safety. Sadly, she never sailed again. With a much reduced crew and her interiors dark and lonely, there were rumours that she might even be converted to a wartime aircraft carrier. US authorities seized her on 12 December 1941, days after the attack on Pearl Harbour and America's formal entry into the Second World War, and renamed her USS *Lafayette*. Transferred to the US Navy and to become a high-capacity Allied troop transport, the huge vessel was being converted at Pier 88 when, on 9 February 1942, she caught fire and then, overloaded with firefighters' water, she capsized and was lost. Beyond salvage, she was cut down, pumped out and righted, and then laid-up until the war's end when she was declared surplus. In the end, in 1946, the brilliant *Normandie* was sold to local Port Newark, New Jersey scrappers for a scant $161,000. She was then just eleven years old.

two

The Post-War Atlantic

The Second World War was devastating to all Atlantic shipping lines. While Cunard was left with eight passenger ships, the Italians had only four survivors and the French Line had but two passenger liners. The defeated Germans had none. In 1938, there was the *Paris*, *Ile de France*, *Lafayette*, *Champlain* and, of course, the *Normandie*. But for the French Line, both the *Paris* and *Lafayette* had burned at Le Havre in the late '30s, the *Champlain* was sunk in 1940 and the *Normandie* burned out and sank at New York two years later.

In 1945, as the war in Europe ended, CGT's Paris offices had to scramble to revive its Le Havre-New York service, vacant for over five years. Interim sailings were run by the *Ile de France*, but still in very basic, very austere troopship form, and assisted by assorted other French passenger ships – the *Colombie*, *Athos II*, *Indochinois* and *Marechal Joffre*. But actual regular resumption of regular service was left to a most unlikely ship, the 7,700-ton passenger-cargo vessel *Oregon*. A pre-war ship, she had quarters for thirty-eight passengers, but from 1945 and by doubling the berths in each stateroom, her capacity increased to seventy-six. Basically a freighter, this ship and a sister, the *Wisconsin*, maintained the otherwise prestigious run to and from New York for two years. The two ships carried, in fact, a combined total of 5,200 passengers in 1946, which represented a mere 1 per cent of all Atlantic passenger ship traffic. Obviously, CGT management, along with the firm support of the French government, looked to resurrection and restoration. By 1948, competition was already increasing amongst larger Atlantic liners: Cunard had the *Queen Mary*, *Queen Elizabeth*, *Mauretania* and were building the *Caronia*; the Dutch had the *Nieuw Amsterdam*; and the *America* was then the largest liner flying US colours.

An immediate attempt by the French was also something of a temporary measure. Generally used on the Le Havre-Caribbean run in the 1920s and '30s, the 17,000-ton, 720-passenger *De Grasse* was re-commissioned, after having been sunk in 1944, to restart luxury service on the North Atlantic in July 1947. She was, of course, instantly popular and was booked to capacity on almost all sailings, even in deep winter. Then, as if called on an urgent rescue mission, the hugely popular *Ile de France* was back in commercial service in the summer of 1949, superbly restored, with two instead of the original three funnels and with her kitchens in tact. But better times followed. By the summer of 1951, having been given the German liner *Europa* as post-war reparations, the French had a new flagship: the fully refitted, gloriously restyled 51,000-ton *Liberte*. CGT was back in its stride, both a serious competitor as well as an apt representative of the French nation. At the end of 1951, CGT was carrying 79,200 passengers or 11 per cent of all Atlantic travellers.

Directors at the Paris headquarters were concerned for the future, however. The three liners were already deep in middle age – the *De Grasse*, dating from 1924; the *Ile de France*, 1927; and the *Liberte*, 1930 – and would need to be replaced by the late 1950s. The new 20,000-ton *Flandre* was added in 1952 and she aptly replaced the elderly *De Grasse*. Furthermore, America had introduced the brilliant *United States* that same year. Large, very modern and well appointed, the 53,300-ton ship was also the world's fastest liner, a distinction

Classic luxury: the first class ballroom aboard the *Ile* following her 1948–49 refit and reconditioning. (Author's Collection)

that in itself lured additional passengers. And on every voyage, she called at Le Havre. She was a blazing competitor. In addition there was word that the Americans might build a sistership to the *United States* for the late '50s. Then there were other nagging rumours such as that Cunard was already beginning to think of a replacement for their aging *Queen Mary*. The French had to move, to think, to plan for the future.

Gabrielle Diamont was secretary to the superintendent of Pier 88 in New York of the French Line. It was the early 1950s and the French, reviving service following the bleak, devastating days of the Second World War, had two big liners at the time, the *Ile de France* and the *Liberte*. In an interview made over fifty years later she remembered that:

We were getting a third ship, a brand new liner, built especially in France. She was the *Flandre* and she was commissioned in the summer of 1952. There was great excitement, anticipation, a sense of pride. But the ship was a big embarrassment – she broke-down on her maiden voyage from Le Havre to New York. Flags were flying and horns were sounding, but the new ship was powerless. She just sat in the lower harbour. Tugs had to pull her to Pier 88.

The first class dining room aboard the *Ile de France* included Lalique chandeliers and round-back chairs made slightly smaller in scale to enhance the overall size of the room. (Author's Collection)

Left To much regret, especially in France itself, the *Ile* was sold to Japanese shipbreakers early in 1959. Before being broken-up, however, she was used as the set piece in the Hollywood disaster film *The Last Voyage*. (Author's Collection)

Left A reproduction of an enamel pin from the *Liberte*. (Author's Collection)

Left The German *Europa* was seized by the Allies at the end of the Second World War, in May 1945, and eventually given over to the French as reparations, to become the *Liberte*. Here she is seen at Le Havre in 1950, preparing for a westbound voyage to New York. (Gillespie-Faber Collection)

Right New York's Luxury Liner Row in 1958. From left to right are the *Britannic*, *Queen Elizabeth* and *Mauretania*, all Cunard; the *Liberte*; the *Olympia*, Greek Line; and the *United States*, United States Lines. (Port Authority of New York & New Jersey)

Right Another gathering along Luxury Liner Row. From top to bottom: *United States*, *Liberte*, *Georgic*, *Queen Mary* and *Media*. (Port Authority of New York and New Jersey)

Above A view at New York from June 1960. From top to bottom: *Media*, *Caronia*, *Queen Mary*, *Britannic*, *Liberte*, *America*, *Saturnia* and *Constitution*. (Port Authority of New York and New Jersey)

Opposite, top right The first class main lounge aboard the *Liberte* had been de-Germanised and restyled in unmistakably grand French ocean liner decor. (Gillespie-Faber Collection)

Opposite, centre and bottom right The *Liberte*'s twin funnels were heightened during a 1953–54 winter refit and became two of the tallest ever on an Atlantic liner. (Gillespie-Faber Collection)

Right End of the line: the classic *Liberte* being scrapped at La Spezia in Italy in the spring of 1962. (Author's Collection)

Caribbean-bound: the sisters *Antilles* (left) and *Flandre*, shown at Le Havre when both near-sisters were used on the French Line run to the West Indies. (Philippe Brebant Collection)

The smart-looking *Antilles* berthed at San Juan in 1968. (Author's Collection)

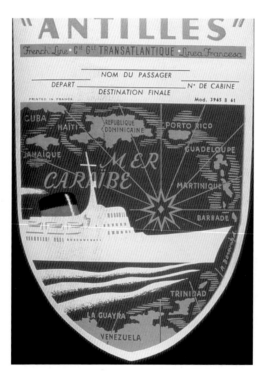

From left A colourful cruise brochure cover for a Carnival-in-Rio voyage. (Author's Collection)

Baggage tag from the French Line's Carribbean service aboard the *Antilles*. (Author's Collection)

The French Line also maintained passenger services from Marseilles as well as Casablanca. (French Line)

Opposite An artist's rendering of the *France*, created in 1959, but without the wings attached to the two funnels. (Cronican-Arroyo Collection)

The 600ft-long *Flandre* was different – she was diesel-driven. The larger *Ile de France* and *Liberte* used the still customary steam turbines. But the new diesels on board the 19-knot ship failed – and several times. The passengers grew impatient and unhappy, the crew were overworked and the French Line itself was deeply embarrassed. Recalled Mrs Diamont:

> The *Flandre* was docked on the south side of Pier 88, just across from *United States* Lines' Pier 86. The liner *United States* was big, hugely innovative, immensely successful and the world's fastest ocean liner. She was the pride of the American nation. But next to her, the *Flandre* – the intended pride of France – seemed small, insignificant, far less than a gleaming ambassador of modern France. So, the superintendent of Pier 88 ordered that the ship be moved, to the north side of the pier, and out of the shadow of the triumphant *United States*.

The idea of a big, new, post-war French liner actually first emerged as early as December 1947. Management felt strongly that the New York run would remain very important. By 1951, the Paris Home Office revealed that the *Ile de France* and *Liberte* were merely 'temporary vessels used in a transitional service' and that new, more competitive tonnage was necessary. Thoughts were realistic and continued that such a new French liner or liners would sail 'hand in hand with aircraft'. A government official said in 1953, 'France is under an obligation to consider, now, the construction of a large transatlantic liner, which should come into service by 1958, when the *Ile de France* and *Liberte* are close to retirement.'

The first serious thoughts, proposals, even preliminary designs were made in 1952. Initially, ideas varied considerably, however. There was talk of twin 35,000-ton liners. Then there were ideas for a 1,300-passenger, 25-knot ship, then a larger 2,000-passenger, 25-knot liner and finally, larger still, a 2,000-passenger, 30-knot ship. There was even a study of reconditioning the otherwise brand new 20,000-ton *Antilles*, then just completed for the Le Havre-West Indies service and a near-sister to the *Flandre*, and using her on the more demanding

A poster celebrating French Line's Caribbean service. (Author's Collection)

New York run. There was considerable debate, discussion as well as disagreement, and therefore delays in Paris, both at CGT headquarters and in government offices (after all, the State would pay as much as 83 per cent for such a new liner).

Finally, the 2,000-passenger, 30-knot idea was selected, using no less than the eighth hull configuration that was proposed and the fourteenth plan for the internal layout. The new super liner was intended for as many as twenty-two crossings per year. To be named *France*, the plans would be based on thirty years of experience, beginning with the *Ile de France*, but especially based on the *Normandie*, but would also include all technological advances. She would, as examples, have stabilizers, complete air-conditioning, soundproofing, a fully welded hull, a light metal superstructure, eight boilers (instead of the twenty-nine fitted on board the *Normandie*) and consume as much as 45 per cent less fuel than her great predecessor. Every contemporary passenger comfort was considered: the ship's daily newspaper, *L'Atlantique*, would be fed by the latest and fastest news services, on board television (100 black and white sets, but only five with colour reception) and in the staterooms of the 500 first class passengers telephones with direct connections to shore.

On the occasion of the maiden voyage of the new Dutch flagship *Rotterdam*, a 38,000-tonner introduced in September 1959, *Newsweek* magazine was very optimistic about the future of Atlantic liner travel. They reported to their millions of readers:

> The *Rotterdam* is being followed on the stage by a scene-stealer, the French Line's 55,000-ton *France*. With other superliners on the way, *France*'s debut will spark a battle of ocean monarchs for the booming passenger trade. Congress, with President Eisenhower's approval, is expected to appropriate about $118 million next year for a sister to United States Lines' *United States* and $86 million for a trans-Pacific American President super liner. And in Britain, a 55,000-ton replacement for the *Queen Mary* is planned.

Both American projects failed to materialize, of course, and Cunard's was bound for great revision.

Expectedly, the construction task was given to the illustrious Chantiers de l'Atlantique at St Nazaire. With the keel laying set on 7 November 1957 and the launching done on 11 May 1960, the *France* actually spent ten months longer on the slipway than the similarly sized *Normandie*.

three

Creating a Super Liner

The building of the 66,300-ton, 2,000-passenger *France* was in fact a personal project of President Charles de Gaulle. He saw the $80 million ship as a lavish morale builder to the French people and for a country that had lost something of its international standing and which was about to shed another troublesome colony, Algeria. Like the illustrious *Normandie* in the Depression-era 1930s, this new *France* was to be 'the modern embodiment of all that is France' – technologically, mechanically, decoratively and certainly gastronomically. More seagulls would indeed follow this French liner than any other ship on the Atlantic. *New York Times* food editor Craig Claiborne would later proclaim that her first class Chambord Restaurant was the very best French restaurant anywhere!

Some 100,000 workers, their families and spectators witnessed the launching of the *France* at St Nazaire in the late afternoon of that May day in 1960. President de Gaulle watched intently as his wife named the giant ship. A crowd of 100,000 witnessed the launch that included a formal blessing of the ship. At precisely 4.15 in the afternoon, Madame de Gaulle cut a red, white and blue ribbon releasing a special bottle of Magnum champagne that slammed into the brand new hull. A crew of 240 was aboard the *France* at the time, under the command of Captain Herve Le Huede, former master of the *Normandie*.

Eighteen months later, she left the shipyard for her sea trials, attaining a top speed of an exceptional 35.21 knots. 'At New York, in the late 1950s, engineers from the *Ile de France* and *Liberte* were always keen on visiting the *United States*, which was often at adjoining Pier 86,' remembered Captain Ed Squire, a New York-based maritime expert. 'Mostly, they wanted to see her otherwise off-limits engine spaces. There were rumours that the new French flagship would try for a speed record, perhaps capture the Blue Ribbon from the Americans.'

The French Line formally accepted the ship on 6 January 1962 and, following a gala pierside charity ball for 1,400, she set off from Le Havre on a sort of shakedown cruise to the Canary Islands. On her return, in the Bay of Biscay, she passed the thirty-two-year-old *Liberte* on her way to the scrapyards in La Spezia in Italy.

The France entered Atlantic service on 3 February with a gala departure from Le Havre for New York. The future seemed bright, but in fact she would sail for CGT for only twelve years and seven months. On her first voyages, she was exceptionally free of any malfunctions – there were no 'teething problems' so often a part of a new ocean liner's first months. According to Squire:

The *France* was the highpoint of the new generation of liners. She was very much the ship of the 1960s. If she had been built in the '50s, she would have been ahead of her time, but she was perfectly suited to the so-called 'Swinging '60s'. Her accommodation was much improved over other big liners of the time and was said to be the finest on the Atlantic in that decade. She was designed to appeal to a wider range of passengers, travellers who might sail one way and fly the other. She had to offer a special experience, almost something unique, and so be competitive in a different way than, say, the Cunard *Queens* or even the *United States*. The French had made up their minds to regain the era, but in a more contemporary way, of the great *Normandie*.

There were several miscalculations, however. No one, including the French Line, expected the airlines to get the upper hand on the Atlantic and get it so quickly. The takeover was abrupt, dramatic, irreversible. So in hindsight, it is a pity that the *France* did not have an outdoor pool or pools and vast sun decks so that she might have been used more in alternative cruising. She might even have had a Magrodome, a glass ceiling covering the pool area and which can be opened and closed, and which was used on the *Oceanic* just three years later, in 1965.

'Vive le *France*!' This cry may have made grammarians shudder in 1962, but it so happened that 'le *France*' is a ship and all words for ships – *bateau, paquebot, navire* – are masculine in French. Attention toward the new liner, not the least of it in France itself, was huge. Because of the recent arrival of jets on the Atlantic and quick, devastating inroads into passenger ship traffic, one French newspaper headlined the ship's delivery:

This maritime thoroughbred of the seas is the biggest bet of recent years. She is the belated successor of the unforgettable *Normandie*, adding her two winged funnels and pure mathematical curves to New York's skyline at a time when prophets of doom can see no future for the super liner in competition with 6-hour jet crossings of the Atlantic.

The year before, in 1961, Cunard scrapped a plan to build a new 75,000-ton liner, dubbed the *Q3*, and with the classic three classes. The decision was not final, of course, and plans were reworked into the more sensible, 66,000-ton, two-class *Q4*, which finally emerged in 1969 as the *Queen Elizabeth 2*.

The French, from almost all corners, were not as seriously interested in competing with the jet. Instead, the role of the *France* was to be a grand, very comfortable floating hotel that created a 'long weekend at sea' to and from Europe. The French Line was also sensitive to the tastes of the all-important American passenger ship trade. One Paris-based executive explained:

American passengers travelling by sea tend to follow their 'flag' – that is Americans of Italian origin take Italian ships, Americans of British origin take

Artist's rendering of the *France* from 1961. (French Line)

Cunarders and so forth. The trouble is, Frenchmen never migrated to the United States in large numbers to create similar traffic for the French Line today. So, the French Line must appeal to a more general clientele and to offer speed as well as its French cuisine and traditional atmosphere of France.

Another French Line executive added:

Today, speed does not cost enough to warrant our imposing a six- or seven-day trip on a passenger. With a fast ship like the *France*, an American businessman, for example, need only lose two working days on his trip to Europe and, in return, he will gain a rest and a vacation in a luxury hotel. The design of the *France* is based on combined facilities for work as well as relaxation – rather than the overwhelming splendour for the vanishing trans-ocean race of the 'idle rich'. Then, of course, there is the tourist class passenger, who can take a sea trip and enjoy huge baggage allowances without wasting his whole vacation just getting there. And like other major steamship companies, the French Line has an exchange agreement with airlines so that a passenger can go by both sea and air on a roundtrip ticket.

The corporate and business trades were still seen as important. Captain Georges Croisile, master of the *France* from her commissioning, added:

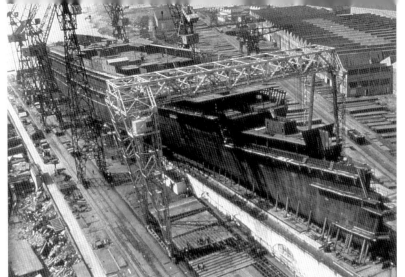

Clockwise from above

The towering bow. (Cronican-Arroyo Collection)

Early construction at St Nazaire. (French Line)

Constructing the bow section. (Gillespie-Faber Collection)

A section of the stern is lifted into place. (Cronican-Arroyo Collection)

From left The lettering for the name *France* is being applied on the starboard side in this view dated April 1960. (Cronican-Arroyo Collection)

This view of the bow also conveys the mastery of French shipbuilding. (Cronican-Arroyo Collection)

Down the ways – the *France* is waterborne for the first time. Her baptism! (Cronican-Arroyo Collection)

A few years ago, companies made a point of sending their big men by air. But now they've realized the importance of cushioning the executive. He needs time to write his reports or, if nothing else, to collect his thoughts. And so, if he can have four or five days in a good hotel for the same cost, so much the better.

Said naval architect Bill Deibert:

The *France* was one of my favourite ocean liners of all time. She was, of course, the last true transatlantic liner. The *QE2* has so often, but incorrectly, I think, been given this title. The *France* was designed from the start to spend much of her year on the Atlantic, as much as nine to ten months, sailing between Le Havre, Southampton and New York, and a short winter season in cruising, mostly from New York to the Caribbean. The *QE2* was created for far more of an even balance, in my opinion. She had a balance of 6 months on the Atlantic and six months in cruising.

Indeed, the French were confident – and very pleased. And from the start, from the trials and first voyages, she seemed to be pure perfection. Captain Croisile noted:

She answered her helm beautifully. She is a particularly docile ship – yes, much more so than my previous command, the *Liberte*. All ships are like women. The *Liberte* was docile too – as long as you were steering her in the direction she wanted to go. But the *France* is different – she is the kind of girl with whom a man simply cannot keep falling in love at first sight.

During her tests, the *France* also proved she knew when to stop – 'a rare feat in a woman,' added the captain. Going from 'full speed ahead' to 'full speed astern', she came to a halt in seven times her own length and, even under such treatment, she 'positively refused' to vibrate. In another test, she listed only very slightly when her helm was thrown over at full speed – and no crockery was broken! Captain

Clockwise from above

The great stern section. (French Line)

The bow comes into form. (French Line)

The vast hulk of the ship has come into place in this dramatic aerial view from 1959. (Cronican-Arroyo Collection)

The *France* is almost ready for her gala, much publicized launching. (Cronican-Arroyo Collection)

Croisile concluded on the subject of early performance, 'I have never seen a ship handle so well in her first trials.'

After reaching an astounding 35 knots during her sea trials, she averaged a very impressive 31 knots on her westbound maiden voyage. Almost immediately there was speculation, even rumours, of a French bid for the Blue Riband. Once at New York, however, Captain Croisile was quick to dismiss the possibility. 'If we did take the record, the *United States* would come right back with her reserve speed and retrieve it,' he said.

Along with her maiden voyage passengers, writers and travel agents and longtime loyalists to the French Line appraised, reviewed, but often also severely criticized the new flagship. One satisfied guest reported, 'She is more a palace than a ship.'

Maiden voyage passengers and visitors goggled at the luxuries aboard the $80 million floating masterpiece. The first class suites were especially impressive, with their large windows, tapestries of French chateaux and some which included private dining rooms. Others were impressed with the patio on the top deck of the ship and which included wrought-iron bars and eight doors from eight penthouses. The teenagers' playland had every amenity – from a milkshake bar to a bowling alley. But about the most dramatic space was the entrance for the Chambord Restaurant, the grand first class restaurant done in circular design. The room was done in gold with enhancing golden murals. Upon entering, passengers descended the twenty-one steps in full view of all other guests. 'It's the kind if staircase every woman dreams of coming down, wearing a gorgeous gown,' commented one maiden voyage passenger.

Some reviews were, however, not as positive. A staff member with forty years at the French Line's New York office commented, 'This is a 1962 ship. You can't go back to the old days. She will be the last of the great liners. But about the *France*, I have mixed feelings – feelings of nostalgia, regret and confusion.' A travel writer said, 'The new *France* is a stately, elegant creature, who is designed for leisurely travel in this rocket ship age. And yet she is a glittering, modern creature made of plastic, metal and glass. There is not one scrap of wood anywhere in her construction or interior except the wheel.'

Without those long-cherished woods, the *France* was variously appraised by her maiden voyage guests as being 'cool', 'self-contained' and 'functional'. A longtime French Line loyalist complained: 'It's completely functional, and anything completely functional upsets me. If you're going to be a remnant of the past, for heaven's sake be a remnant of the past. I wanted Louis XV furniture.'

Surprisingly even to the French Line, maiden voyage travellers found the decor in tourist class to be cosier, more imaginative and more tasteful, and even more restrained than in first class. The most popular place was said to be the tourist class smoking room, which passengers called 'warm and intimate'.

A well-seasoned transatlantic couple commented, 'The *France* is not French. It could be from any country. The tapestries and the murals mostly have universal themes, like sunbursts and fish. Even the *United States* has decor about it that shows American scenes.' Another passenger reflected: 'The *France* is wonderfully free of minutiae, free of all those artsy-crafty things, that shipboard clutter. Instead, everything about her is large and everything is basic.'

The 30-knot *France* settled into a glamorous life – eight or nine months of crossings, between Le Havre, Southampton and New York ($420 minimum fare in first class in 1962, $225 in tourist class) and the rest on cruises (the Caribbean mostly, but also Carnival-in-Rio, the Mediterranean, West Africa). Later in her career, she would make two highly publicized trips around the world. She visited varied ports: Cape Town, Bombay, Singapore, Sydney and Hong Kong. On those trips, no ship ever sailed, for example, with her cellars stocked with less than the finest wines. Extra linens had to flown out from Paris and additional five-star chefs joined en route just in case there might be a little boredom in that otherwise splendid Chambord Restaurant.

Ocean liner enthusiast and historian Steven Winograd was a great fan of the *France*. He recalled:

> She was my most favourite ship in my lifetime. When I was twelve, in December 1967, my family and I sailed aboard her on a twelve-day Christmas–New Year's Caribbean cruise from New York. As we pulled down West 48th Street, we had a full view of the ship. Flags were fluttering from end to end. Light snow was falling and the *United States*, *Empress of Canada* and *Europa* were also in port, berthed nearby. It was a night time sailing for the *France*. Like all liners in those days, a Christmas tree was attached to her mast.
>
> Once on board, your heard music such as songs by Maurice Chevalier and there were lots of balloons. You first saw those big floor mats that were marked CGT. Then there were *mousses*, uniformed and hatted, all lined-up and grabbing hand luggage from well-dressed, often fur-coated boarding

The triumphant maiden arrival in New York harbour in February 1962.
(Cronican-Arroyo Collection)

A rendition of the maiden arrival by an unnamed French artist.
(Author's Collection)

passengers. In the lounges, there were big, gala bon voyage parties. Spirits were high, the mood festive. Even though there were no class distinctions on a cruise, it was quiet and demure in the first class section. In tourist class, it was lively and spirited. The outer decks were littered with snow and, together with other youngsters, we made a snowman wearing a French beret. We heard the German band from the *Europa*, which was docked on the other side of Pier 88. The sounds drifted over. We towered above the piers and could look down the funnels of the *Europa*.

'The *France*'s personality, her chic, her great allure made her a great favourite in the 1960s,' added naval architect and passenger ship expert Bill Deibert. 'I think that she did the very best anyone could expect to hold on to the "Transat liner mystique". And she was the longest liner yet built as well. She held that distinction for years, until the 1,132-foot-long *Queen Mary 2* first appeared in 2003.'

A former president of New York City's Ocean Liner Museum Project, Frank Trumbour, added:

She belongs in the Ocean Liner Hall of Fame for the latter half of the twentieth century. Her lines were so beautiful and graceful. Her striking funnels, which were quite revolutionary, 'worked' so well. And, of course, she had the French cache about her. She was far more beautiful than, say, the *QE2*. Those distinctive winged funnels, for example, were like sculptures. Her ultra slim hull and very fine bow gave her exquisite symmetry. And the *France* always remained the same. The *QE2* was always changing, always adding this and that – more exterior cabins, more lifeboats, a new funnel, a reduction of an outdoor pool. Unfortunately, the *France* was not in service as long as the *QE2* and so her impact and her history are different.

four

Luxury at Sea

The late Lewis Gordon began crossing the Atlantic by ship, aboard the likes of the *Aquitania*, *Berengaria* and then brand new *Queen Mary*, in the late '30s. By the '70s, he and his wife had made over 100 crossings. They were very fond of the French Line and, in particular, very much liked the new *France*. Mr Gordon remembered:

> You always met the chic-est and saw the most fabulously dressed women in first class on board the *France*. Like the *Ile de France* and the *Liberte* before her, the *France* had some of the greatest, grandest and most glamorous public rooms – high-ceilinged lounges, Aubusson carpets and impressive stairways.
>
> And the kitchens were justifiably famous. Passengers actually used to vie with one another to produce special recipes that could stump the French chefs. They never did, of course, but sometimes these same items might appear on the regular ship's menu two days later. I especially remember Chicken Subarov, a whole chicken baked in clay and then broken open. On board the *France*, they used one pound boxes of Beluga and served it with a soup spoon. There were three kinds of wine at every table, all of it complimentary from the French Line's private vineyards. And, of course, you could have filet mignon at breakfast. It was true: the French dumped the best leftovers over the sides!

'The *France* had great personality. She was the most luxurious and, in ways, the most celebrated big liner of her time, in the 1960s,' according to Frank Trumbour. 'She had the personality and style of an elegant modernist. She was masked in ways by a traditional exterior (save those winged funnels) while on the inside she was chic, albeit a cool chic given her modern interiors. But overall, she represented continuity of the best French Line tradition.'

In a career that included passenger ships, freighters and New York's famed Staten Island ferry, Captain Ed Squire felt she defined the 1960s on the Atlantic:

> The *France* was very much a ship of her time. She had modern style and a great sense of comfort. She was so like the innovative *Normandie* in ways and also like the *United States*, but actually better than both. She had excellent deck layout, for example, and wonderful colouring that suited the times. Her first class dining room was one of the finest rooms ever to go to sea and there was the likes of the superb dual promenade.

Steven Winograd also appreciated the stance of the *France*. 'She was elegant and so beautifully balanced on the outside,' he said. 'She always seemed to be ready for take-off. She was very much an Atlantic Flyer. And those funnels were like Air France at sea level.'

In the late 1950s and early '60s, transatlantic liners were very much still being created. Britain added the *Empress of Canada*, Holland had the *Rotterdam*, West Germany introduced the converted *Hanseatic* and *Bremen* and Italy produced one of the most stunning, the *Leonardo da Vinci*. And yet more were in the works: a new *Kungsholm* for the Swedes, the *Sagafjord* of Norway, the *Michelangelo* and *Raffaello* under the Italian colours and the *Shalom* for Israel. Each brought in something of an individual and often different style.

Maiden departure from New York in February 1962. (Gillespie-Faber Collection)

Left Returning from her inaugural cruise to Le Havre, the brand new *France* passes the soon-to-be-scrapped *Liberte*. (French Line)

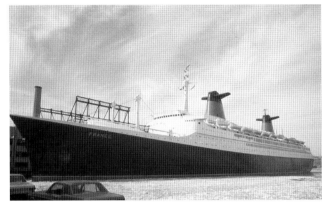

Right Madame de Gaulle has named the ship – it is officially the *France*! (French Line)

Left The world's longest liner resting between voyages at New York's Pier 88. (Norman Knebel Collection)

Left Inbound at Southampton in late afternoon. (Richard Faber Collection)

Right Night-time at Le Havre. (Richard Faber Collection)

Left Another view of the distinctive funnels. (Albert Wilhelmi Collection)

From left to right The iconic funnels, which were often compared to Mexican sombrero hats. (French Line)

Departing from New York with a Moran tug at the bow. (Albert Wilhelmi Collection)

Sleek and elegant, the *France*'s rear funnel. (French Line)

Left Passing the *Canberra* at Southampton. (Robert O'Brien Collection)

Right Arriving at New York on 30 May 1974. (Author's Collection)

Left Dramatic aerial view at sea. (French Line)

Right Wintery afternoon: the outbound *France* passes the famed Lower Manhattan skyline. (French Line)

'In the beginning, from 1962, the modernist interiors of the *France* did not appeal to me,' added Frank Trumbour. 'They still do not today. However, compared to what was modern in the 1950s and '60s, on board ships such as the *United States* and *Cristoforo Colombo*, they had an elegance about them. They screamed "sparse but chic".'

Alternately, naval architect Bill Deibert appreciated the interiors of the *France* in the 1960s:

The word 'elegance' was quickly fading from most vocabularies by the '60s. Instead, it was a new age of mod, fab and plastic. Strobe lights became something of a symbol for an age. The world was changing and it was changing in ocean liner design and decor as well. And the changes came quickly. The new age was one of discotheques and flashing lights. There were drastic changes in fashion, music, interior decoration. The *France* somehow

managed to retain a sense of elegance, especially in her first class spaces and staterooms. She was a hybrid of decor, but still very much a great liner. The French have always been innovators. Even if her furniture was, in some cases, quite different, even bizarre, she still managed to have a classiness about her. Even if the age of white tie and tails and flowing shimmering silk dresses was all but over, the *France* was still elegant. And, of course, she always had the very best cuisine and service afloat. The *QE2*, which first arrived seven years later, was too much of a dual-purpose-built ship to be a 'true' liner in the old sense. Both on the outside and within, the *France* was the last great Atlantic liner.

The original interiors were misunderstood, highly misrepresented and maligned in their verbal interpretation by many. My opinion is that they were simply 'avant guard'. Sure they were different and sometimes very different, but only some of the actual furnishings were over the top. Some were simply not attractive. But overall, especially in first class, she was a great beauty and

Outbound and passing the Statue of Liberty on a summer's afternoon.
(Port Authority of New York & New Jersey)

The superb Chambord Restaurant. (Albert Wilhelmi Collection)

The first class promenade. (Albert Wilhelmi Collection)

The first class Smoking Room. (Albert Wilhelmi Collection)

The indoor pool for first class. (Albert Wilhelmi Collection)

The Grand Salon, also in first class. (Albert Wilhelmi Collection)

The bedroom of the superb Normandie suite. (Albert Wilhelmi Collection)

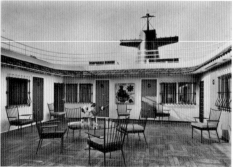

The Patio in first class. (Albert Wilhelmi Collection)

The bedroom of a first class outside double. (Albert Wilhelmi Collection)

you could feel an 'expensiveness' in her decor that was not generally evident in, say, the *QE2*, except possibly in the Princess and Queens Grill Rooms. I think that the *France*'s interiors were more like the *Michelangelo* and *Raffaello*, but minus the velour. Those two ships were elegant examples of '60s decor, especially in their Grand Salons. They were tasteful and civilized and beautifully done. But other rooms in these ships were odd in furniture, their type and colour and use of materials.'

During the '60s, the rebellion was against establishment. The establishment had certain defined notions of ethics, conduct, sex and what was considered elegant and tasteful. This extended to architecture, decor, furniture, certainly music and the arts. In general, I feel that the *France* and her interiors walked a fine line. She maintained the established elegance, but with a touch of the mod, even odd. Times were, of course, changing and she reflected this. It was new age, even for great, big ocean liners. The designers and decorators of the *France* attempted to reflect these changes, the new era, but they were also very cautious. Comparatively, the *France* was not on the scale of the *Normandie*'s positive acceptance as an absolute 'show stopper'.

Steven Winograd added:

The interiors were generally a disappointment with the exception of the Chambord Restaurant, the Riviera Lounge and the Fountainebleau Lounge. I especially remember the Riviera Lounge Bar, which stretched for 69 feet and was the longest at sea. I also recall the most elegantly dressed women and also wearing the most fabulous jewels as they came down the main staircase of the Chambord Restaurant. It seemed that everyone's eyes were trained on their arrivals. Comparatively, even the food seemed to receive less attention. It was a show unto itself. I also remember my father sitting in the Riviera Lounge after dinner and smoking Havana cigars, which were available to Americans on French liners despite the Cuban embargo of the 1960s. She had far too much peg leg furniture and chairs. She did not look French or even French Line, but like something from another planet. But the food and the service made her. On cruises, the waiters even packed lunches for excursions ashore. And she had this great sense of glamour. When you stepped aboard, you were in *France*! Her only equal for food and service at New York in those days was the *Oceanic* of Home Lines. The *France* was, in many ways, the *Normandie* of her time. That great style was still there. Out of over 100 different liners, she was the most exciting I've ever sailed aboard. And especially to see her at night, moored in, say, a Caribbean harbour. She was lighted from end to end, sparkling and twinkling. She was like a big diamond bracelet.

With twin levels, the great theatre. (Albert Wilhelmi Collection)

The tourist class main lounge. (Albert Wilhelmi Collection)

The Smoking Room in tourist class. (Albert Wilhelmi Collection)

A three-berth tourist class cabin. (Albert Wilhelmi Collection)

Left Anchored off Martinique in the Caribbean during a cruise. (French Line)

Right Departing from New York. (Author's Collection)

Left Luxury Liner Row, 1965. From top to bottom: the *Constitution*, American Export Lines; the *United States*, United States Lines; the *France*; the *Raffaello*, Italian Line; and the *Queen Elizabeth*, Cunard Line. (Port Authority of New York & New Jersey)

Left A winter's day at New York, February 1973, and a final gathering: the *France* (left), *Queen Elizabeth 2* and *Michelangelo* are together. (Port Authority of New York & New Jersey)

Right Modern and almost stark, a foyer on board the *France*. (French Line)

The unique circular design of the original Chambord Restaurant in first class. (Author's Collection)

The tourist class restaurant. (Albert Wilhelmi Collection)

The twin-level theatre. (Albert Wilhelmi Collection)

The splendid first class library. (French Line)

The glorious first class Smoking Room. (French Line)

The first class promenade. (Albert Wilhelmi Collection)

The Grand Salon, also in first class. (Albert Wilhelmi Collection)

The cheerful children's playroom. (French Line)

Above, left French Line was noted for its impeccable service – and, of course, what was perhaps the finest food at sea. (French Line)

Above, right Even the souvenirs were most interesting – such as the funnel-like ashtray. Today, it is a prized collectible from the last of the great French liners. (Richard Faber Collection)

'The *France* was often criticized for the starkness of her interior decor, but really she was quite elegant and sleek,' added Charles Howland, a New York City-based ocean liner collector and historian. The *France* was modern, very contemporary, from end to end. The Chambord Restaurant was round, had illuminated rotunda and a majestic twenty-one-step grand staircase as an entry. A small, but very select grill room adjoined. The library was also circular and the theatre sat 664 passengers on two levels. There was an indoor pool for first class voyagers that was highlighted by a great crystal chandelier and a glass-roofed pool for tourist class. The gym had an adjoining squash court. Some superior first class cabins faced onto a unique Spanish patio, located in the middle of the Sun Deck and between the two great funnels. The very elegant top penthouse suites, named Normandie and Ile de France, consisted of an entrance hall, pantry, private dining room, living room and two bedrooms. The kitchen staff consisted of 180 cooks, sauce and pastry chefs, rotisserie cooks, head waiters and wine waiters. The fine crystal collection comprised of 4,800 water and wine glasses. Then there were 22,000 pieces of china and 25,500 pieces of silverware. On a five-day crossing, 11,750 tablecloths and 50,000 dinner napkins were used.

France dinner menus are great collectibles even to this day. First class dinner menus always appeared in the smoking room each afternoon and then dinner in the Chambord was full of delights – with as many as 250 different items listed on the oversized, artistically covered, foldout menus. There were the tantalizing likes of Iranian caviar on ice that vied with *pistachio terrine* of young rabbit, *Medallion de turbot de Boulogne* with *Delices de sole d'Ostende Marguery*, *Carre d'agneau de la Pointe-de-Grace Florian* with roast Maryland turkey stuffed with Ardeche chestnuts and prized *beef steak au poivre* France style. The dessert menu included Brazilian iced dessert, Sicilian pistachio ice cream and a *bavaroise Nesselrode*. To accompany these, over 400 different wines were kept in the on board cellars. CGT noted that on each five-day crossing, the daily dinner consumption for some 3,200 passengers and crew was the equivalent of slaughtering eighty head of cattle, sixty calves and forty sheep. Then there was also 35 tons of fresh vegetables, 200 kilos of caviar and 90 kilos of frogs' legs.

Very early in her career, the *France* had a very special 'guest' on board for a westbound crossing to New York. Softening the then often chilly diplomatic relations between France and the United States, President John F. Kennedy and his wife Jacqueline made a hugely successful visit to Paris, which included several meetings with President de Gaulle himself, in May 1961. One of the results was to send none other than the *Mona Lisa* to the USA for a very special exhibition in Washington. Although not especially well received by the French themselves, the exchange took on months of detailed planning, all akin to a major military manoeuvre.

Months later, at daybreak on 14 December and under heavy guard, the *Mona Lisa* was quietly and gently lifted from the wall of the Grande Galerie of the Louvre and inserted inside a special, high-tech travelling case, which was then placed in a wooden crate. Museum workers dressed in matching overalls slowly loaded the box inside the back of a medium-size, steel-fortified truck. Inside the vehicle, the crate was mounted on cushioned springs designed to guard against vibrations that might shake bits of the pigment from the picture's surface. Escorted by three police cars, the truck then departed the museum garage. A squadron of six police motorcycles formed a protective cordon around the convoy and accompanied the painting along the 110-mile route from Paris to the *France* at the dockside at Le Havre. Under secret surveillance throughout the journey, the wooden crate was later loaded on board, where it was bolted to the floor of Cabin M79 and then covered with a thick, dark grey wool blanket. Normally, the spacious first class cabin had a rate of $2,000 per person for the five-night passage. Nine French guards plus two officials from the Louvre and another escort making for a party of an even dozen travelled with the painting.

Clockwise, from above As seen from the top decks of the departing *Leonardo da Vinci*, the *France*, *United States* and *Independence* form a background in this 1965 view. (French Line)

The great funnels seen on a winter's afternoon in 1968. (Author's Collection)

Loading cargo at New York's Pier 88 in 1972. (Author's Collection)

Awaiting departure in June 1973. (Author's Collection)

Later, after departing from Le Havre and making an unusual short stop at Southampton, the *France* was revved up to her usual 30 knots and sped west for New York. None of the 1,800 passengers on board knew that they would be part of a historic crossing, travelling with the *Mona Lisa* on her first voyage to the New World. But later, passenger suspicions were aroused. First class travellers were refused entrance to a certain passageway and this was coupled with reports of rather unusual security. Quickly, rumours circulated that the *France* was transporting some strange military-like, perhaps even secret, device – possibly nuclear – of the Cold War. But finally, and against the strong wishes of the French escorts, the ship's captain revealed the truth – the passengers were travelling not with a Cold War weapon, but the illustrious *Mona Lisa*. Afterward, to mark the occasion, the captain ordered fine wines and champagne. Quickly, apprehension turned to celebration. Suddenly, there were *Mona Lisa* costume parties, games and a series of celebrations in the ship's bars and lounges. The liner's chefs, butchers and pastry makers prepared appropriate delicacies – roast beef Leonardo, salad Mona Lisa and parfait La Gioconda. Grand dinners, especially in the exquisite Chambord, seemed to go on longer than usual and often well into the night. The mood was celebratory and cheerful. One night, a mischievous passenger even managed to slip past the heavy security to place a pair of women's shoes outside the *Mona Lisa*'s otherwise well-guarded cabin. On another occasion, a couple in one of the finest first class suites sent a specially printed invitation for the *Mona Lisa* to join them. The voyage of the great artwork was seen, of course, as a great symbol of French-American friendship and cooperation.

The *France* reached New York harbour on the morning of 19 December and was unusually welcomed by spraying fireboats and extra tugs. As she made her way to Pier 88, an especially high number of passengers lined the outer, upper decks and waved tiny French flags. The *Mona Lisa* was, it was reported in local newspapers, given a 'queen's welcome'. Of course, the publicity for the ship itself and for the French Line was immense. 'It was like the maiden arrival all over again,' said a French Line employee in the company's New York City office.

After being secured to the north side of Pier 88, four uniformed French Line crew members carried the *Mona Lisa* into the Grand Salon as the ship's public address system played Musorgsky's *Pictures at an Exhibition*. 'It was all very spiritual,' commented a passenger awaiting his own call to disembark. A forty-five-minute press conference on board the liner followed. The Director General of the Museums of France ceremoniously handed the painting over to the special representative of President Kennedy. The ship's pastry chef had baked a sugar-and-butter cream cake in the image of *Mona Lisa*, and that culinary masterpiece was then placed atop the real lady's travelling case. It was the only *Mona Lisa* reporters would get to see that day.

Offloaded onto Pier 88 later that morning and then stowed in a high-security van, President Kennedy ordered that a Secret Service guard be locked inside the back of the van with the painting. Again, the transport process was planned with military precision. Police sharpshooters were strategically placed on rooftops along Manhattan's West Side and along the Hudson River end of West 42nd Street. Crossing under the river and over to New Jersey, the Lincoln Tunnel was cleared of all traffic. With sirens screaming and red lights flashing, the eight-car motorcade, escorted by squadrons of state police, sped through New Jersey, Delaware and Maryland before entering Washington DC. The entire route was so well planned, that the entourage never stopped for a single red light. A wintery ice storm at Washington slowed the final progress, but that night and under further great care, the *Mona Lisa* was safely delivered to the National Gallery. Her voyage was complete.

Afterward, the *France* resumed her normal operations. Jane Bouche Strong made nineteen crossings aboard the liner between 1963 and the ship's final trip in the late summer of 1974. 'There was always the awesome first sight of the ship's prow, like a giant knife blade, in the water at Pier 88,' she recalled:

A typical Transat embarkation was, of course, a flurry of activity. At the pier, a messy commotion of longshoremen handled bags from taxis and cars to a moving ramp, while passengers and bewildered tourists tottered under bon voyage baskets up separate canvas-sided gangplanks. At the top was a double line of little bellboys in snappy red jackets with rows of brass buttons and black caps. There were called 'mousses', a name the derivation of which I never grasped. They took whatever we passengers were carrying and escorted us to our staterooms.

After leaving our things, including our small dog, in the cabin, we went direct to the dining room to select, with the help of the matire'd hotel, our table for two at the second sitting. This done, we took a quick look at the temporary passenger list outside the purser's office to see if we had any friends on board. (A day or two day later, the final list appeared in one's cabin.)

Returning to our unlocked cabin (one rarely locked doors then), we found flowers, pre-ordered Champagne and finger sandwiches, and our well-wishing guests, all piling in at once. The farewell festivities lasted a brief hour, until the claxon sounded and insistent loudspeaker announced, '*Tous les visiteurs a terre!'* [all visitors ashore].

Mrs Strong continued her recollections of the last of the grand French liners:

Soon we set about the business of unpacking – I arranged my evening clothes in the order in which I planned to wear them, saving the dressiest for the gala, while sipping the last of the Champagne. We turned on the radio built into the vanity, which on Sunday mornings played the music of bells of French country churches. Then three thunderous blasts of the claxon – and we were off! Shortly after departure, the glass doors to the *salle a manger* were thrown open and everyone went down for that tremendously anticipated first meal. There were warm greetings between the waiters and the *fideles*, and bottles of red and white wine were opened at every table. Sometimes, we ordered fancier wines, for which we paid a surcharge at the end of the voyage. French Line food was justifiably famous – fiery *steak au poivre* in Armagnac sauce, buttery lobster with Cognac and luscious *pommes dauphine* were among the seemingly limitless choices. Anything you wanted that was not on the menu could be ordered for the next meal. After lunch, it was time for a little reconnoitering: checking on the films that would be shown, selecting a book in the library, poking into a chic boutique, prudently making a hair appointment well in advance of the gala and finally, selecting our deck chairs.

Outbound in the Hudson River on a summer's afternoon. (Author's Collection)

With a New York harbour tug and barges in the foreground. (Author's Collection)

Two icons: the *France* and the Empire State Building. (Author's Collection)

Two more icons: the *France* and the twin towers of the World Trade Centre, in another view from June 1973. (Author's Collection)

Above A rendition of the liner at New York. (Author's Collection)

Left Young ship enthusiast Pine Hodges on the left as the *France* is berthed at New York in the early 1970s. (Pine Hodges Collection)

In her dozen years of French service, there were the headlines, the news items and, of course, the occasional incidents – the delayed sailings, the tugboat strikes, dockers' strikes, crew strikes. She was always of at least some interest. During her five-day maiden voyage stay at New York's Pier 88, the French Line's offices at Rockefeller Centre reported it was receiving over 1,000 calls per day with inquiries about the newsworthy super liner.

In July 1962, a French seamen's strike caused an Atlantic sailing to be cancelled and the ship unexpectedly placed in dry dock. But instead, the strike was then cancelled at the last minute and the ship sent off on a revised schedule. Consequently, at New York, she made a record turnaround – arriving at 9 in the morning and then sailing fourteen hours later at 11 that same night. Some 600 passengers had arrived and 1,400 were embarking on the return. Dockers and French Line staff worked at an almost frantic pace. Some 4,414 bags of mail, 90 tons of freight, a dozen passenger automobiles and 2,600 pieces of baggage were offloaded. Later, as the liner sailed past the late night skyline of Manhattan, she had taken on 1,000 bags of mail, 6,000 pieces of baggage and forty cars. In addition, she had been hurriedly replenished with 4,000 tons of fuel oil and 50 tons of provisions. Her turnaround broke the previous record at New York, set by the *Queen Elizabeth* in January 1961. She had been 'turned around' in 16½ hours.

Another notation from that maiden summer of 1962 showed a record 11,000 visitors at Pier 88. Both the *France* and the *Bremen* were sailing at midnight. The *France* departed with 1,865 passengers and had 7,500 visitors while the *Bremen* sailed with 1,139 passengers and having had 3,500 visitors. That fall, the French Line announced that the *France* had 'surpassed all expectations,' carrying 80 per cent of capacity in her first six months of service. She had carried 35,000 passengers and had, on occasion, been booked to 99 per cent of capacity. A year later, the French Line reported that the *France* had earned $22.7 million in twelve months of passenger and cargo revenues.

In the ensuing years, news stories continued regarding the French liner. She struck the pier at Southampton in a squall, while wealthy first class passengers reported $25,000 in jewels missing from their luggage. Then, quite embarrassing, $400,000 of heroin was discovered hidden in pipes in a boiler room upon her arrival in New York harbour. She also established another record: arriving with 2,036 passengers, thirty-six more than normal top capacity, in September 1964. Days later, the *Queen Elizabeth* arrived with 2,197 aboard. Then more news: While undocking, a US Navy ship bumped into the *France* at Pier 88.

By late 1968, with the retirement of both Cunard *Queens*, the *France* became the largest liner in the world. But within a year, Paris newspapers in particular were reporting that the seven-year-old *France* might be retired and even scrapped. The French government was rapidly losing interest in supplying $40 million a year in subsidies to operate French-flag passenger ships. Alone, the *France*'s subsidies were amounting to some $10 million. The government cited the high cost of operations (especially the expensive, highly unionised crew of 1,100), the increasing challenge of airlines and that less than a quarter of her passengers were French citizens.

Strikes and work stoppages continued. In the fall of 1970, two voyages were cancelled when 150 restaurant waiters demanded

A French cartoon of the *France*. (Cronican-Arroyo Collection)

an extra thirty minutes of overtime each day. Waiters and busboys blocked gangways on board until the strike was settled, but as 4,800 passengers had to seek transport elsewhere. Andre Morell, a one-time first class cabin steward, recalled:

> By the late '60s, the *France* was becoming a spider web of unions, union power struggles and union intrigues. The on board atmosphere for the staff was no longer pleasant. Individual freedoms as well as pride and performance in job were disappearing. I finally left the *France* sooner than I expected.

Steven Winograd and his family were aboard the Christmas Holiday cruise from New York to the Caribbean in 1967. 'We had a storm at Nassau,' he remembered. 'Anchored offshore, the *France*'s tenders were rolling and pitching. The weather was soon worse. Soon, the *France*, along with the *Queen Elizabeth* and the *Federico 'C'*, could not retrieve their passengers. Everyone was waiting on piers. It turned into a fourteen-hour day.'

Intended to make twenty-two roundtrip crossings per year, in reality the *France* averaged only fifteen. While she carried 700,000 passengers between 1962 and 1974, some 114,000 of these were on cruises. While 80 per cent of all passenger traffic on the Atlantic crossed by ship in 1950, the jet blatantly intruded in 1958–59 and it plunged to 32 per cent by sea. But by 1973–74, less than 2 per cent of all trans-ocean travellers were using ships. The *France* was struggling – and struggling harder than ever before. Then fuel oil prices soared from $35 to $95 a ton, also in 1973, and, for the following season, the liner's maximum speed was reduced to 24 knots and the crossings extended from five to six days. A one-way 'youth fare' of $150 was introduced to help fill empty berths in tourist class. But then to complicate matters, there were continuing industrial problems. 'Unions had been strangling CGT from the very start, from 1962,' reported a former *France* purser. 'Working conditions by the late '60s had become very tense. Union leaders were not seamen and they did not understand. They often made the worst decisions and often had the most unrealistic demands.'

The *France* made exciting news when she set off on her first around-the-world cruise in January 1972. It was billed as the 'most opulent world cruise in history'. She sailed off with 1,100 passengers on board, including 375 Americans, on a lavish ninety-one-night circumnavigation – and with fares soaring up to $100,000 per person. The planning took years: twenty-seven ports of call and 224 shore excursions – ranging from a $7 tour of Mombasa in Kenya to a $1,395 nine-day overland side trip through India and Nepal. And then the icing on the grand cake: a last-minute approval for a forty-eight-hour visit to secretive Communist China. The excursion would even come on a historic note – the day after the history-making visit by US President Richard Nixon to Beijing. Passengers left the flag-bedecked *France* at Hong Kong and then travelled by special train to Canton and later trained to Singapore and rejoined the ship.

Fares for the 41,000-mile journey started at $5,065, but climbed to $99,430 for the sumptuous, upper-deck Ile de France Suite, consisting of two bedrooms, a sitting room and private dining room. Over fifty passengers took extra cabins, at $7,500 each, to hold wardrobes and luggage. One lady took an extra cabin for her 250 dresses.

The French Line pulled out all the stops. The on board programming included extra movies in the theatre, fashion shows and lessons in cooking, wine selection, painting and French language classes. There was also a stable of twelve guest lecturers, including a stock market analyst. Cabaret performers were added for evening performances and then changed during the voyage.

Many of the guests were loyalists of the *France*. One Canadian woman had sailed aboard the ship thirty times in ten years. A Florida couple, longtime repeaters, referred to the ship as their 'winter home'. A Brazilian family brought along their own maid, cook and tutor for their two grandchildren.

Headline-making, this lavish fling on the *France* was created to celebrate two anniversaries: the ship's tenth anniversary and the centennial of Phileas Fogg's fabled voyage around the world in eighty days. The ship's bartenders concocted a Phileas Fogg Cocktail and actor Claude Dauphin, who served as the Cruise Host, donned a Phileas Fogg costume on special occasions. And there were plenty of those. There were fifteen formal balls, including one in memory of Fogg's chronicler, Jules Verne. In preparation, passengers were offered lessons in the minuet.

One of the major attractions of such a cruise aboard the legendary *France* was the mouth-watering opportunity to savour 270 meals and in 'the best French restaurant in the world'. In preparation, the ship's larders were specially packed with the likes of 300,000 bottles of wine and a full ton of caviar. Chef Henri La Huede went public and promised never to serve the same dish twice. Indeed, a great feat – alone, there were seventy-five items on the daily luncheon menus. 'The only problem with this trip will be to handle all that food,' said a widow from Chicago. 'But I think I've solved it. I bought all my clothes two sizes too big.'

Just as when the great *Normandie* sailed to Rio for Carnival in February 1938 and then again a year later, that inaugural world cruise of the *France* was well documented, making for often interesting reading. Passengers mostly ranged in age from sixty and upwards, and one wit described the on board atmosphere as 'less glamorous and more geriatric'. Word had actually leaked out that thirty-one would-be passengers, mostly elderly, died between the time they booked and the ship began her journey. The vacancies, it was said, were quickly filled as waiting lists were 'pages and pages long'.

The entertainment, it was later reported, included feature films, but mostly vintage titles, reruns of American sitcoms and drama series on the ship's in-house television system and rather sombre night time lounges frequented by small handfuls of waltzing couples. The gleaming disco was, as expected, all but deserted. Some guests bemoaned the fact that the great, amenity-filled *France* did not, in fact, have an outdoor swimming pool.

couple brought along cases of the family champagne and handed out bottles as tips. A Texas widow brought along her harp while another single lady set gold cigarette boxes about her suite, but each filled with $500 in crisp dollar bills for daily gratuities. But one couple were obviously worried about the cuisine. They brought along cases of their favourite Boston baked beans, fish balls, cranberry jelly and even peanut butter.

Passengers on the world voyage could also make use of the ship's complement of four doctors and a dentist (normally, only two doctors were aboard) and received medical care at French government prices, a bargain when compared to American standards. The *France*'s medical contingent, prepared for the ailments of the aged, had some early surprises. On the first day out of New York, three women inquired about abortions.

But while often booked to the very last berth in tourist class, the *France* lost money and then more money. Her benefactor, the Ministry of Transport in Paris, lost interest. Her annual $14 million subsidy would be better used, so they thought, for Air France's supersonic *Concorde*. This craft was the new symbol of 'all that is France'. In the end, the French government under President Jacques Chirac decided to end all maritime subsidies effective 1 July 1974. Finally, in September, on the eve of a seamen's strike demanding no less than a 35 per cent increase in wages, the *France* was decommissioned. Her last two crossings were cancelled and the ship mothballed in the Canal of Le Havre, a backwater berth. Afterward, her future was one of rumour: it was reported variously that the Chinese, Soviets, Arabs and even Club Med wanted her. She was, in fact, sold to TAG, a firm controlled by Saudi Arabian millionaire Akram Ojjeh, in 1977, but rather oddly for intended use as a floating casino and museum of French design and culture, and moored off, of all places, Daytona Beach, Florida. The sale price was $16 million, but the idea never came to pass. In the summer of 1979, Norwegians bought her for $18 million and dramatically transformed the indoor, transatlantic *France* into the outdoor, tropical *Norway*. Thought of redoing the liner in a French shipyard was dropped when costs were 60 per cent greater than those offered by Germany's Hapag Lloyd Shipyard at Bremerhaven. Under tow, the former *France* left Le Havre on 18 August 1979. By the following May, she began sailing in Caribbean waters and, for years afterward, ranked as the largest cruise ship in the world.

Tight squeeze: passing under New York's Verrazano-Narrows Bridge. (Author's Collection)

While many passengers were very interesting, there were no celebrities – at least recognisable ones – on board. But the expected opulence and glamour prevailed. One French woman wore a ring so heavy, it was widely reported, that she removed it at every meal so as to lift her knife and fork. Another woman brought along fifty designer evening gowns. A Swiss couple paid over $900 just to bring their beloved poodle along, while a family in one of the top suites brought along twenty-five cases of their favourite whiskey. A French

The Lower Manhattan skyline begins to fade on a summer afternoon in July 1973. (Author's Collection)

The great name in large mounted letters on the upper deck. (Author's Collection)

Dead calm in the summertime North Atlantic. (Author's Collection)

Above Along the Sun Deck in the mid-Atlantic. (Author's Collection)

Left, from top

Sparkling lights on the horizon: night-time during a Caribbean cruise. (French Line)

During a world cruise, the grand liner at Hong Kong. (French Line)

The great name in large mounted letters on the upper deck. (Author's Collection)

The great ship tendering in the Caribbean. (French Line)

five

Sailing to the Sun: The Norway

In 1990, when French President Mitterand visited Oslo, he stopped at the National Maritime Museum. But the large model of the *Norway* was thoughtfully moved out of sight. Presidential advance teams evidently thought it might be an indiscreet reminder of the ship that was once the ocean-going glory of *France*. She was then a highly successful cruise ship, but sailing for the Norwegians.

'The *France* was very, very fortunate to become the *Norway*,' said Frank Trumbour. 'Although altered, much of what was the *France* was kept in tact, at least in the early days with Norwegian Cruise Lines. A new generation of cruise passengers could therefore enjoy much of what had been a chic ocean liner.' Captain Ed Squire stated:

If she had not gone to the Norwegians, the *France* might well have been laid-up for years, just like the *United States*. The Norwegians saved her and gave her a great second career. As the *Norway*, she was the great forerunner, the trial run, the master plan, that led to today's mega cruise liners. But in reality, no one could ever have guessed the huge success of the *Norway*. She went well past expectations. Her conversion was superb in almost every way. The only error was that she should have been diesel-ized from the start. Keeping the original steam turbines was a mistake in my opinion.

There was, however, another blemish according to Captain Squire:

The two decks that were added later in 1990 were not especially well done. It was created in light steel and lacked high quality. You could hear easily from room to room, for example. Even the furnishings in those newly added cabins was of lower quality. Altogether, it tarnished the image of the *Norway*.

'I first saw the *Norway* in 1980, in her new colours – the all-blue hull and the blue and white stacks,' remembered Charles Howland. 'She looked brand new and immaculate. Earlier, in the 1960s, I had seen the CGT brochures, which of course captivated me and aroused my imagination. And she had those wonderful stacks.'

According to Bill Deibert:

The transformation of the *France* into the *Norway* was quite amazing. It was ideal for the time. It was an extraordinary achievement technically to turn this ship 'inside/out' and make her a famous, very profitable cruise ship for a growing market. This ship was very instrumental for further increasing interest in the growing cruise market of the early 1980s.

Steven Winograd added:

I felt somewhat sad when the *France* became the *Norway*, but it was a great reprieve for that otherwise unwanted ship. By the late 1970s, she might even have been scrapped. I recall going aboard, walking through the new Norwegian Cruise Lines' interiors and feeling dismayed. In ways, she was less dignified, even cheapened. But later, when NCL added those two top decks, she was really demeaned. She almost stopped being the former *France*. The excitement of that great ship was all but gone.

Left The enormous bow. (French Line)

Outbound on a cruise.
(French Line)

Warm waters – cruising
in a sunny Caribbean.
(French Line)

Above During her 1972 world cruise, the *France* is seen
here at Sydney, Australia. (Peter Plowman Collection)

As part of her cruises
from New York,
the *France* called
occasionally at Port
Everglades, Florida. In
this view from 1969,
we see the *Frederico
'C'* and then the *Queen
Elizabeth*, the former
Cunarder that was to
be made over as a local
museum and hotel.
(Author's Collection)

Left, from top Sad and lonely, the *France* is laid-up at Le Havre, 1974–79. (French Line)

The former French flagship is towed away to Bremerhaven, West Germany, in August 1979. (Author's Collection)

The great transformation: the indoor *France* becomes the outdoor *Norway* in 1979–80. (Robert O'Brien Collection)

Opposite, clockwise from top left The former French flagship heads for Germany and her reinvention as the *Norway* in the 1980s. (Author's Collection)

A poster celebrating the *Norway* in the 1980s. (Author's Collection)

Viking ownership – Knut Kloster, owner of Norwegian Cruise Lines, takes command. (Author's Collection)

Maiden call at New York in May 1980. (Author's Collection)

At New York on that maiden call. (Author's Collection).

The Biggest Week in the World

THE NORWAY

TIMELESS GRACE AND ELEGANCE

Right, from top The rebuilt stern section of the *Norway*. (Author's Collection)

The iconic World Trade Centre in Lower Manhattan. (Author's Collection)

Opposite, from far left A Moran tug seems dwarfed by the mighty *Norway*. (Author's Collection)

Flag-bedecked and with horns and whistles sounding, the blue-hulled *Norway* looked majestic and beautiful as she sailed along the Hudson River. (Author's Collection)

In her new life, the *Norway* had become far more efficient: she operated at a more conservative 18 knots, reducing her fuel consumption by some 2,000 tons per week; five bow thrusters were added for easy handling; deck spaces were opened while most public rooms and many cabins were redecorated; and there was the thoughtful addition of two large tenders, named *Little Norway I* and *Little Norway II*, carrying 400 passengers each and for easy landing in Caribbean ports. Furthermore, her crew was reduced in size from 1,100 to some 900 (alone, engine room staff dropped from 167 to 52), while her original French Line maximum capacity of 2,044 had increased to a maximum of 2,560 by 1990. She repaid her costs and investment by NCL within six years, by 1986, and had a 90 per cent occupancy factor during the 1980s. She was not surpassed in size, however, until 1987 by the 73,100-ton *Sovereign of the Seas*, ironically also built at St Nazaire for Royal Caribbean Lines. By 2003, St Nazaire broke all records by delivering the 151,000-ton *Queen Mary 2*.

When Captain Hans Meeg first saw the mighty *France*, the world's longest liner, at her New York pier in the 1960s, he was very impressed. But he was even more excited in the summer of 1981. While working as junior officer on a reefer ship – or more romantically, a 'banana boat' – he discovered that the former French flagship, by then restyled as the *Norway*, the world's largest cruise ship, was nearby. 'She was very newsworthy then,' he recalled. 'I detoured and our small cargo ship met the *Norway* and then we cruised around her for fifteen minutes.' But he could not have realized that he would one day be master of the 2,565-berth *Norway*. He joined her owners, Norwegian Cruise Lines, in 1987. He served in their *Starward*, *Skyward* and *Seaward*, and on board the affiliate Royal Viking Line ships *Royal Viking Sun* and *Royal Viking Sky*.

The starboard side of the newly refitted liner. (Author's Collection)

Blue was an appropriate colour for the new super liner of Caribbean cruising. (Author's Collection)

Coming from a family of lighthouse keepers, the young Meeg was infatuated with ships and the sea at a very early age. 'My first boat as a young boy was actually an old lifeboat that we converted into a small sailing ship,' he recounted while in the upper-deck comfort of his luxuriously spacious office-sitting room aboard the fifteen-deck *Norway*. We met in August 1995, during a celebratory cruise highlighting the liner's French Line heritage and her special place in ocean liner history. During a week-long cruise to St Thomas, St Maarten and a private Bahamian out island, there were maritime slide lectures and films, on board guided tours, special cocktail parties and even the sale of luxury liner memorabilia, much of it from bygone French liners. There were postcards and posters, silver ashtrays, foldout deck plans and even a porcelain replica of one of the *France*'s distinctively winged funnels.

'Five friends and I travelled around the Norwegian fjords in our converted sailboat,' the captain added. 'We were called the "Blue Navy" because we painted our boat blue. Later, during the summer months, I worked on a Norwegian trawler. This cured me of seasickness forever! I first went to sea in the early '70s, sailing on one of those "banana boats".'

Surely, the job of commanding the enormous *Norway* was quite different, indeed a great contrast. He said:

Every day is a challenge. We have 930 crewmembers, for example, and from no less than thirty-five different countries. And we handle 10,000 pieces of luggage every Saturday, for example. And then just bringing the ship in and out of Miami requires great skill. She takes twenty minutes just to turn in the inner harbour basin and, being steam turbine, she can't stop as fast. The newer, diesel-driven *Seaward* can stop in seconds. The *Norway* takes ten minutes!

'She is still a very solid ship, of course, despite her thirty-three years of age. Her keel plates were made to last for fifty years,' said Captain Meeg. He added:

The main engines are still the same from the 1979–80 conversion, but getting parts sometimes takes up to a year. Sometimes, of course, we make parts ourselves. The old, unused turbines are still below and sometimes we use them for spare pieces. We can still reach 24 knots [the original top speed was 30 knots], but that would be very expensive. At 21 knots, we use 400 tons of fuel per day. But these days, and with newer propellers, we average 17 knots going south and 14 heading north. She is a still a heavy ship. After we added the new, upper deck, for example, we placed five tanks of concrete in the bottom. We will be making more changes during the big, seven-week overhaul that is scheduled to begin on 31 August 1996.

A spraying fireboat leads the way as the ship sails along the lower Hudson River. (Author's Collection)

Above The restyled, former Chambord Restaurant. (Norwegian Cruise Lines)

Left The large group of ocean liner enthusiasts aboard the *Norway* in 1996. (Author's Collection)

Above The superbly refitted Club Internationale. (Norwegian Cruise Lines)

Left Another view of the Club Internationale. (Norwegian Cruise Lines)

The *Norway* offered every modern amenity: outdoor pools, a basketball court, lido restaurant, two decks of shops, a large casino, gymnasium, showrooms, bars and the first mega-showtime revue on the high seas with no less than two dozen singers and dancers. There was even a Roman Spa.

At the Spa, passengers might just have forgotten that they were actually at sea, in fact aboard one of the world's largest and most famous cruise ships. It was a setting of peace and calm, utter serenity, and of marble statues and Cleopatra-style settees, torch lamps and terracotta floors and, of course, those classic Roman columns. Located down on Dolphin Deck, it seemed to be from another world and a place where passengers could relax, indulge and luxuriate.

Guests could get away from the pace, the sometimes hectic mood of cruise ship life just above – away from the limbo contests and bingo games, the cabarets and casinos and those leggy, feathered dancers in those after-dinner revues. 'It is all peace and serenity here,' said Rebecca Cuxton, the Spa's manageress. 'We maintain a minimum noise level. There's no running about. There are no children, no portable music players, no cameras, no videos.'

Spa services (in 1995) had a wide range. There were the likes of twenty-five minutes of aromatherapy ($43), a forty-five-minute men's energizing facial ($50), a fifty-five-minute slenderizing body wrap ($55) and something dubbed a three-part mud mood therapy ($190). Generally, there was a $25-a-day charge just to use the Spa facilities – the whirlpool, the plunge baths, the steam room. A dozen therapists and a receptionist manned the facility, and some 400-500 passengers per cruise used it. 'We get lots of repeater passengers and lots of business people, who need to "de-stress",' added Ms Cuxton. 'We have a wide range of ages and an especially big demand for morning treatments.'

The prices were all a-la-carte and so various treatments could be put together. There was also a $125 rate for couples, which included two twenty-five-minute massages as well as use of the Spa for the rest of the cruise. The Spa was also linked to the ship's two restaurants with special dietary and healthy living menus for lunch and dinner. In the Spa itself, healthy living breakfasts were available until 11 o'clock and included an array of fresh juices. There was even something called a 'power juice'!

A relaxing facial, a soothing massage, a dip in a warm, foamy, bubbly pool – what could be better? One guest added, 'The only thing better than the Spa is to be aboard the *Norway* itself!'

The great promenade deck was an entertainment venue in itself. (Norwegian Cruise Lines)

One of the great stairwells aboard the then world's largest liner. (Author's Collection)

Evening departure from Miami in January 1981. (Author's Collection)

Opposite, clockwise from top left The popular aft pool.
(Norwegian Cruise Lines)

Looking aft on starboard side. (Author's Collection)

The popular aft pool. (Author's Collection)

Fun under the sun! (Author's Collection)

Her name in large letters, which were lighted by night. (Author's Collection)

Opposite, from left Those great funnels. (Author's Collection)

Afternoon at sea in the tranquil Caribbean. (Author's Collection)

Late afternoon departure from Miami. (Author's Collection)

Looking aft on the starboard side. (Author's Collection)

The bow of the 1,035ft-long super liner. (Author's Collection)

The Norwegian colours are proudly displayed. (Author's Collection)

A rare visit
to New York.
(Author's
Collection)

Moored off Great Stirrup Cay in the Bahamas. (Author's Collection)

Night-time in tropic waters. (Author's Collection)

Cato Christensen was staff captain of the *Norway* for two years, between 1999 and 2001. 'As the *Norway*, the ship still had great ambience. It was very special. She had a different feeling than other ships,' he recalled. 'There was history, even great history, just in the walls. Even in some of her public rooms, such as the Club International, there was a special tone. Simply, she was like no other ship.' He added:

The *Norway* was strong and solid, and built like very few other ships. Her watertight doors, for example, could be individually operated and closed in thirty seconds. They were so advanced for a ship designed in the '50s and built in the early '60s. Although the forward engine room had been removed by NCL, she had her original steam turbines. But I think Kloster regretted not converting her to diesel during the big refit in '79–80. She was, of course, quite a different ship to handle and to experience. She had delayed manoeuvres. There were forty-five-second delays. It was always quite an experience to handle this 1,035-foot long ship in, say, the Miami turning basin.

'But she was a great ship to the very end,' continued Captain Christensen, adding:

Of course, we needed extra staff in the engine room because of those steam turbines. The crew liked, but mostly loved her. They felt, quite rightfully, that she was a ship of history. They worked extra hard to make her work. We had one man continuously painting, for example, in the galley just to keep it looking spotless and fresh. About 85-90 per cent of the crew always returned to her. Her US Public Health scores were sometimes on the edge, however, because of her age and we'd always lose 2 points just because of that. Most of Deck 5 was still original, for example, and so were many of the suites. In the Captain's Office, there was still a button on the desk that connected directly to the pantry for instant service. As Vice Captain, my cabin had been the 'dog house' when the ship had a large kennel. The kennels themselves and that famous New York City fire hydrant were gone, however. By 2001, we still had great passenger loads and lots of repeater passengers. One guest came with his butler and had a big suite for four-six cruises at a time. But once the butler sent the chauffeur and the car off, but with all the luggage as well. So, the chauffeur had to fly to the first port of call, St Thomas, with the luggage and the clothes.

While her Caribbean voyages were very successful (averaging 83 per cent occupancy in the 1980s), she was sent farther afield on occasion. In July 1984, she sailed from Miami via Philadelphia to Southampton and then ran a series of summer cruises to the Norwegian fjords and

The *Norway* sailing from Miami on 2 September 2001. (Andy Hernandez Collection)

Her splendid, easily recognisable funnels. (Author's Collection)

the North Cape. Two years later, she made a special American coastal cruise – seven days from Miami to Wilmington, Charleston, Savannah, Jacksonville and Freeport.

In December 1989 she had a special charter steeped in ocean liner nostalgia: a gastronomic cruise marketed heavily to the French, thirty-three top chefs joined the ship to create the finest in shipboard dining, in fact recreating the era of the French Line and the *France* itself. French classical musicians added to the theme cruise. A great success, these French charters were repeated in 1990 and '91. The cruise in 1990 was actually marketed to French travellers under the ship's original name, but it was not formally changed.

New York City-based ocean liner memorabilia dealer and collector Richard Faber was aboard the *Norway*'s French gourmet cruise in December 1990:

It was a week-long voyage of extraordinary excess. For one week, we had top, top quality food. There were many French passengers on board and the chefs on board represented most of the top restaurants in France. There was excess caviar, specialties of every kind and $500 wines. Each meal was eagerly anticipated. Along the enclosed promenades, there were great bowls of caviar, fine pates, the most exquisite culinary creations. It was actually decadent, almost vulgar. But in the Caribbean, we had the worst weather for the entire trip. There was, however, a great mood and high sense of excitement on that sailing. Really, it was out of this world. It wasn't cheap, of course, and was actually double the normal seven-day fare. Many passengers wore the finest clothes and this added glamour to the voyage. The ship was re-christened as the *France* for the entire week and even the top-deck lettering spelled out *France*.

In 1995, a long cruise from Miami to the Mediterranean, including a stop at Cannes for the famed Film Festival, was planned and reportedly included temporarily renaming the ship as the *France* and even repainting the funnels in French Line colours. But interest paled and the idea was cancelled. In the summer of 1996 she crossed from Miami via New York to Southampton for a refit. She called at Le Havre for the first time since 1979, had some 6,000 visitors (including many former French Line employees and crewmembers) and then sailed off at midnight to fireworks and a cheering crowd of 100,000. In 1998 she had nearly six months in Europe, from April through October, cruising the Mediterranean first and then up to Northern Europe. She was back in Europe a year later as well.

six

Twilight on an Indian Beach

Many enthusiasts, including some diehard fans of the *France/Norway*, felt that, even at over forty years of age, she should be saved – becoming a moored hotel, a museum, an entertainment centre, even a casino. But saving liners, especially very large ones, has traditionally been filled with problems and usually financial ones. The *Queen Mary*, moored in southern California, has generally been an exception – she endures to this day. Also, the Japanese have saved the 1930-built *Hikawa Maru* and, far more recently, the *Rotterdam* of 1959 was prepared for preservation in 2006–07. And now added to the last is the *Queen Elizabeth 2*, which will serve her Dubai owners, from late 2008, as a combination hotel and entertainment complex while moored on Palm Island. (As a revision of plans, the *QE2* is serving as a moored hotel at Capetown beginning in 2009.)

Advertised as a sentimental last voyage, the *Norway* left Miami and then New York for a North Atlantic cruise ending at Southampton in September 2001 – just days before the devastating terrorist attacks in America of 11 September – on what was to have been her final sailing. Over 300 ocean liner enthusiasts were aboard. The grand finale was five farewell cruises, departing from Le Havre and Marseilles, under charter to the French. Afterward, she was to go into Asian cruising for Star Cruises. 'She was tired, getting old and there were problems with power. There were problems even during the departure from New York,' recalled Captain Ed Squire. 'She hit the opposite pier while undocking and was belching lots of smoke. She drew 34ft of water and was nearly at the bottom of the Hudson. Tugs were pushing hard.'

But during the crossing, which ended at Southampton, Norwegian Cruise Lines rethought their decision and decided to continue sailing the *Norway*. 'I think that NCL was being rather greedy,' added Captain Squire. 'She had lots of deterioration by then and it was an endless task to make replacement parts for her. There were also questions about her US Coast Guard certification.'

The great decline in travel following the September 2001 attacks left the *Norway* struggling. She was often half full and rates for her week-long cruises plunged to as little as $199 (or as low as $28 per person per day) on some sailings. But even greater troubles were ahead. On 26 May 2003, having just arrived at Miami from a seven-day cruise, a main steam line exploded and caused considerable damage. Several crew members were killed, others injured and the event made news everywhere. The image of the *Norway* was tarnished and Malaysian-owned Star Cruises, the owners of Norwegian Cruise Lines, saw the event as a 'bad omen'.

Captain Christensen added, 'NCL lost almost all interest in her after the explosion. Star Cruises, the new parent of NCL, lost interest as well. Everything actually changed with Star. The mood was different. There was no chance of seeing her get expensive repairs and returning to service.'

The *Norway* was soon laid-up and then sailed empty to Bremerhaven for inspection and the inevitable rumours of repairs. But the overall investment in a ship that was then forty-two years old was far too great. She remained mostly at Bremerhaven for two years, until July 2005 when she went out East. She had been used as a training school for crews for new NCL cruise ships. Only temporary repairs would

At Miami: a late afternoon departure in 1981. (Author's Collection)

Outbound from Miami. (Norwegian Cruise Lines)

Another view of departure. (Author's Collection)

Her forward section. (Author's Collection)

be made, it was said, and the ship moved under direct Star Cruises' management for one-night gambling cruises from, according to differing reports, Hong Kong, Singapore or Port Klang in Malaysia. Subsequent reports that she would be going for scrap led to opposition from the internationally recognised Green Peace Organisation. The ship was, they reported, filled with considerable asbestos. She was back, if briefly, in worldwide news. In the end, she fled – departing unrepaired from Bremerhaven, arriving at Port Klang on 10 August. Out in East waters, there were further rumours that she might be restored as a one-night cruise ship or become a moored casino. There was also reports that she would go to China, to become housing or an industrial accommodation centre. Further rumours flourished – a firm based in Quebec wanted to restore her as a combination transatlantic liner and cruise ship, Dubai was said to be interested for use as an entertainment centre and hotel, Amsterdam investors had similar ideas, and expectedly the French might feel nostalgic and use her, most likely as a casino at Honfleur and not far from her one-time berth at Le Havre. 'Honfleur officials owned the local casino, feared the competition and so blocked the idea in the end,' reported a French journalist. In the end, the much-faded, rusting *Norway* was sold to Indian scrappers and renamed 'Blue Lady'. She was moved to Alang in India in the summer of 2006 to await demolition.

The *Norway* on a summer cruise visit to the splendid Norwegian fjords.
(Robert O'Brien Collection)

Clockwise, from bottom left Changed funnel markings in the 1990s.

The NCL logo appears.

Stormy seas during an Atlantic crossing.

The new, revised NCL logo in the 1990s.

Undergoing repairs at Bremerhaven.

Another view in dry dry dock. (Robert O'Brien Collection)

Anchored in the Caribbean. (Robert O'Brien Collection)

The *Norway* prepares to depart the Lloyd Werft shipyard at Bremerhaven following a refit. (Robert O'Brien Collection)

A glow in night-time lights. (Robert O'Brien Collection)

At Bremerhaven. (Robert O'Brien Collection)

Laid-up and waiting. (Author's Collection)

Bound for Germany under tow. (Andy Hernandez Collection)

But the Green Peace Organisation re-emerged and the Indian courts were petitioned to delay the ship's demolition. She was, Green Peace officials determined, far too dangerous to the workers at Alang. Several reports of the demolition having later begun proved false.

Frank Trumbour noted:

I suppose that almost any ocean liner buff would wish that any famous liner be saved. The reality is, of course, that not everything can be saved. In a way, the *France* was saved – sailing for many years as the *Norway*. Ideally, if she had been saved as a moored keepsake, it would have to have been in France, in my opinion, and in her best French Line finery. She will always be remembered for what she was, which was the continuity of the great elegance of the French Line. The original advertisements read 'France Afloat', which is what she was. She was handsome, contemporary, a standard setter for food and service and style.

Many others believed as well that she should have been preserved. Bill Deibert is among them:

She is part of the last surge on the North Atlantic, of the last newbuilds of the late '50s and '60s. Others included the likes of the *Rotterdam*, *Leonardo da Vinci*, *Empress of Canada*, *Shalom*, *Michelangelo* and *Raffaello*. She was part of an army making a last stand for a cause that was soon lost. The North Atlantic liner era was all but over. But the *France* was, in my opinion, the best of the lot. She was number one. She was such a beautiful vessel. From every angle, and just like Catherine Deneuve today, she was stunning. Pure *classique*! I have a film of a flyover that lasts about three minutes with her at full speed. It takes your breath away. I am so happy that I can say that yes, I have sailed on her!

I am sorry to say, however, and like the *Normandie*, the *France* will not be remembered in the same way as the original *Queen Mary* and even the *Queen Elizabeth 2*. Both of those ships had long and eventful careers and so created 'history'. The *Normandie* had a very short career and the *France* sailed only for twelve years under the French Line. But at all costs, I felt the *France/Norway* should have been saved. We have the *Queen Mary* preserved in southern California so why not the *France* and even the *United States*. How many classic cars, trains, warships, even small boats are currently preserved? And how many historic structures, buildings, even homes? The *France*, like the *United States*, deserved to be saved. These ships would be static exhibits and not only of the great age of ocean liners, but to an age of design and style and decor. They deserved to live on.

Left Two maritime icons: the *Queen Elizabeth 2* is arriving as the *Norway* is berthed just behind at a Le Havre pier. (Robert O'Brien Collection)

Right Outbound in her twilight years. (Andy Hernandez Collection)

Left At Southampton: the *Norway* is on the left, the *QE2* to the right. (Robert O'Brien Collection)

Right Farewell to the *Norway*. (Robert O'Brien Collection)

Left The idle liner waiting at Bremerhaven; her fate is uncertain in this 2004 view. (Robert O'Brien Collection)

Right Following the decisive boiler explosion, the *Norway* is being towed from Miami to Germany in the summer of 2003. (Robert O'Brien Collection)

Captain Christensen also greatly regretted her demise as well:

> It is very, very sad that she has been scrapped. She should have been saved, possibly as a museum and hotel, and like the *QE2* in Dubai. This would have been better. Her steel hull was still so strong. It was 2 inches thick below the waterline. We once had a problem undocking. But in the end, there was more damage to the pier than to the ship.

In January 2007 it was reported that the 'Blue Lady' was quiet, empty, untouched and lying on a beach at Alang. Demolition was to begin in March, but then there were further delays. While there were rumours that Middle Eastern, European and even French interests still wanted to save her, it was revealed that her hull was seriously damaged when she was first run aground and beached. It was no longer possible, according to reports from India, to save her and tow her off to some form of resurrection.

By as late as November 2007, the actual scrapping had yet to begin, but Indian officials did allow the ship to be stripped and therefore prepared for the actual dismantling. Furthermore, she needed to be lightened and, on the right tide, be brought closer to shore. While she contains as much as 900 tons of toxic wastes, including asbestos, workers boarded the former *France* and brought off tables, chairs, even chandeliers and mirrors. Much of it will find its way into homes in towns and villages surrounding Alang.

Despite the many warnings of health hazards, the great majority of workers welcomed the 'Blue Lady', claiming that their health was secondary to the need to earn enough money to feed themselves and often their families. 'Forget the toxic fumes and the chemicals, I might die instead in poverty,' said a thirty-three-year-old migrant worker and the father of four, who first settled in Alang in 1993. He lived in one of Alang's congested slums, sharing a single room with eight men. There

From top Laid-up at Bremerhaven 2003–05. (Robert O'Brien Collection)

A dramatic aerial view of the laid-up liner. (Robert O'Brien Collection)

Awaiting demolition: the beached *Norway* at Alang in January 2007. (Robert O'Brien Collection)

lastword@lloydslist.com

Follow your nose

IT IS too late to save the former French transatlantic liner *France* (ex-*Norway*, ex-*Blue Lady*) from demolition but the vessel's many aficionados can still acquire one of its distinguishing attributes — its nose.

The 3.5 m high, four-tonne nose, right, is to be put up for auction along with some of the vessel's internal furnishings at a two-day sale in Paris on February 8 and 9.

It is on display on the Champs Elysées, where Artcurial, the gallery organising the sale, has its headquarters. Artcurial estimates the value of the blue and white stem at €80,000-€100,000 ($102,000-$128,000).

Jacques Dworczak, its owner, saved it from demolition with the rest of the vessel at Alang in India.

He claimed that he had wanted to fulfil a dream to exhibit "the nose of the most beautiful liner in the world on the most beautiful avenue in the world".

Built in 1961 at the Chantiers de l'Atlantique shipyard, *France* made 377 Atlantic crossings under French colours before it was laid up in 1974.

It was subsequently acquired by Norwegian Cruise Lines and operated as *Norway* until May 2003 when its commercial life was ended by a boiler explosion in Miami in which a number of crew members died or were injured.

Clockwise, from bottom left Coincidental to the ship's demolition in far-off India, the former French Line passenger terminal at Le Havre was itself demolished in the winter of 2009. (Philippe Brebant Collection)

Sad sight: demolition has begun in this most poignant view dated April 2008. (Kaushal Trivedi, through P.K. Productions 2008)

Sentimental piece: the 4-ton nose of the *France/Norway* was auctioned-off in Paris in the spring of 2009 and, after finding a buyer, has gone to Deauville, near Le Havre, as a monument of the last of the great French liners.

is no running water and no electricity. He might earn as much as $1 a day for scrapping. But when there are no ships to scrap, and there have been far fewer in India recently, life is very hard for the work crews. They might eat in the open kitchens of the scrapping company or collect scraps of strewn metal or even garbage to sell for their evening meals. While the one-year battle over the 'Blue Lady' was being fought, many other workers were forced to take meagre jobs in nearby factories or running tea stalls. Together, they prayed that the ship would be cleared and the scrapping begun.

Green Peace has claimed that Alang and the scrap companies do not have the technology nor the interest to safely scrap ships. In a report, Green Peace says that thousands of workers in the shipbreaking industry, in India as well as Pakistan and China, have died in the past twenty years due to exposure to toxic wastes and, more specifically, asbestos. Government-suggested safety workshops at scrapyards rarely occur and the workers, most of whom suffer from chronic respiratory ailments, are poorly equipped for their tasks and have no health insurance. According to an international ship scrapping organisation, the 70,000-ton 'Blue Lady' will provide work for some 4,000 labourers. Even the cast-off machinery, furniture and specialty antiques will give a welcome boost to severely depressed Alang. But the benefits brought by the ship come at a serious cost to the workers. 'Ships like the multi-deck 'Blue Lady' are hazardous, of course,' added a Green Peace spokesperson. 'But fires, falling from heights, explosions, small fires and asphyxiation while working in enclosed areas are not the only troubles. Asbestos is the silent killer at Alang.'

As with other famous liners, pieces of the *France/Norway* went to the auction block, to sales catalogues, even to flea markets. Ocean liner memorabilia specialist Richard Faber reported the returns were far less than impressive, however:

The returns were dismal. In fact, the items offered at the annual ocean liner auction at Christie's in New York, in June 2008, did not sell at all. These days, there are very few keen *France* collectors. Like the well-loved *Rotterdam* [retired in 1998 from Holland America Line service], interest in the *France/Norway* has petered away quickly. These days [2009] only the *Titanic*, *Olympic* and, of course, the *Normandie* are big sellers. The best items, including the artworks, from the *France* were actually sold off in Paris in the late '70s and did very well. More recently, it was mostly items from her time as the *Norway*. Some of these items were of little interest while others were in poor condition.

By 2009, the ship was gone. Only pieces of her could be saved, preserved, kept as mementoes of a great vessel. But that February, the bow section of the ship was auctioned in Paris. The 15ft-high, 4-ton nose of the ship went on auction in a two-day sale on the 8th and 9th. Previously, it was displayed by Artcurial, a specialist gallery, in the headquarters on the Champs Elysees. Jacques Dworczak, the gallery owner, had proclaimed that he wanted to display 'the nose of the most beautiful liner in the world on the most beautiful avenue in the world'. Prior to the sale, the value was given an estimated value of between $102,000-128,000. The Sunday sale auction was indeed a success – the bow section fetched well over $200,000.

Disappearing in often great segments, the ship was completely demolished by the summer of 2008. She was gone forever, her last steel pieces hoisted onto the shores of Alang. 'I found it hard to mourn the passing of the *France/Norway* after a wonderful forty-five-year career,' noted Charles Howland in a discussion of the ship in 2007 and soon after the preliminary stripping in Alang had begun. 'She did everything a passenger ship is designed to do – she carried millions of happy and satisfied passengers. She did everything her original designers asked of her. Overall, she was a tremendous success!'

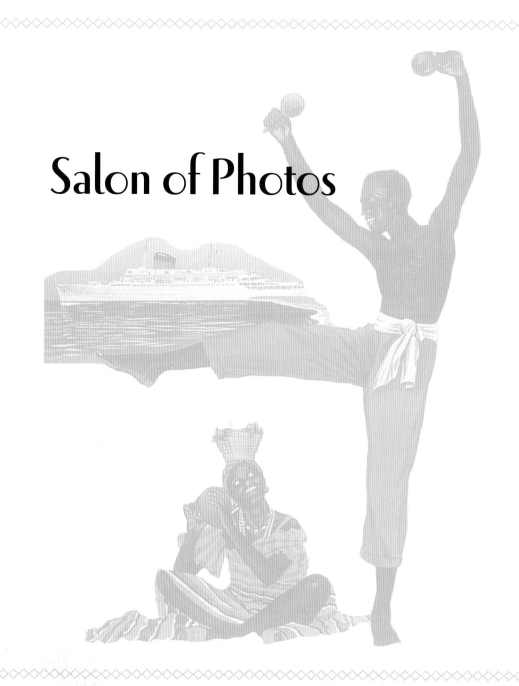

Salon of Photos

The *France* departs from
New York on a wintery
afternoon in 1962.
(Author's Collection)

Afternoon departure from Manhattan. (Fred Rodriguez Collection)

The *Norway* arriving in New York on 5 September 2001. (William Donnall Collection)

At Miami, looking aft from the top of the forward tunnel.
(Robert O'Brien Collection)

While in the Caribbean, an aerial view of the upper decks. (Robert O'Brien Collection)

A sweeping view of the top deck. (Robert O'Brien Collection)

The *Norway*'s final departure from New York on 5 September 2001. (Robert O'Brien Collection)

Moodful evening view in Caribbean waters. (Robert O'Brien Collection)

Two giants at Miami – the *Norway* in the foreground, the *Sovereign of the Seas* just behind. (Jan-Orlav Storli Collection)

Bibliography

Braynard, Frank O., *Picture History of the Normandie*. (Mineola, New York: Dover Publications Inc, 1987)

Braynard, Frank O. & Miller, William H., *Fifty Famous Liners Volume I*. (Cambridge, England: Patrick Stephens Ltd, 1982)

Baul, Patrick J., *Half Century of Cruise Ships in Saint-Nazaire*. (Spezet, France: Coop Breizh Publications, 2003)

Miller, William H., *Picture History of the French Line*. (Mineola, New York: Dover Publications, 1997)

Other titles by the same author

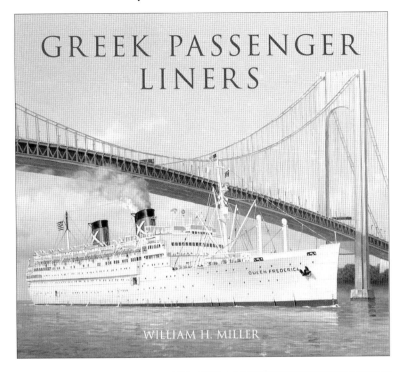

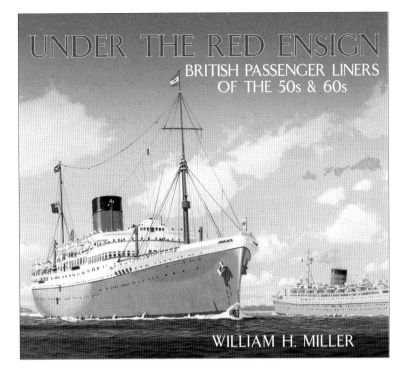

Clockwise from above:

Under the Red Ensign: British Passenger Ships of the 50s & 60s

Remembering the Golden Age of British passenger shipping, when new liners were still being constructed and the finest liners afloat, the Cunard Queens, were at their peak.

ISBN 978 0 7524 4619 6

SS Canberra

Having served in war and peace, this is the story of the famous cruise ship known affectionately as 'The Great White Whale'.

ISBN 978 0 7524 4211 2

Greek Passenger Liners

Relating the history of the Greek fleets that made the world of cruising so exciting over the years.

ISBN 978 0 7524 3886 3

CLASSIC LINERS SERIES

Leviathan: America's First Superliner

BRENT I. HOLT

The story of the *Leviathan* is a fascinating one. She was one of the most popular liners of the 1920s and a ship of many firsts, notably being the first American superliner, and setting the stage for future successes with other famous passenger vessels such as the *America* and the *United States*. Although of German origin, the '*Levi*' was popular and became a household name across America and other parts of the world. Her interiors were stunning and she was an engineering marvel. She had an adventurous career that Brent Holt captures wonderfully in this beautifully illustrated history.

ISBN 978 0 7524 4763 6

Visit our website and discover thousands of other History Press books.

www.thehistorypress.co.uk